ROUGH GUIDES

POCKET **ROUGH GUIDE**
COPENHAGEN

written and researched by
TARANEH GHAJAR JERVEN

CONTENTS

Introduction   4

Best places to explore on two wheels..................... 5
When to visit.. 6
Where to.. 7
Copenhagen at a glance 8
Things not to miss..10
Itineraries..18

Places   23

Tivoli and Rådhuspladsen...24
Strøget and the Inner City 30
Slotsholmen..44
Nyhavn and Frederiksstaden......................................50
Rosenborg and around 60
Christianshavn and Holmen...70
Vesterbro and Frederiksberg......................................78
Nørrebro and Østerbro 88
Day-trips...98
Malmö 106

Accommodation   111

Essentials   119

Arrival 120
Getting around..120
Directory A–Z 122
Festivals and events 126
Danish 127
Chronology...128
Small print...130

COPENHAGEN

Once a low-key underrated city, for the past decade, the Danish capital has been showered with superlatives, with polls claiming it to have the best quality of life and rating its citizens the happiest people on the planet. If that wasn't enough, accolades for its cuisine, metro, cycling and design have followed, and Danish TV dramas continue to bring its Nordic style, gritty architecture and photogenic inhabitants into millions of living rooms. Despite its new-found glory, Copenhagen remains a relaxed, homely place where visitors quickly feel at ease; and while all this cool contentment doesn't come cheap (for tourists and locals alike) the "great Dane" has quite definitely arrived as one of Europe's outstanding destinations.

Exhibition Hall in Louisiana Museum

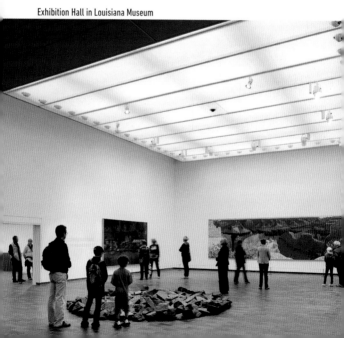

Cycling in Copenhagen

Part of Copenhagen's appeal is its hybrid nature, a unique blend of mainland Europe and Scandinavia. The city looks as much to London, Berlin and Amsterdam as it does to Stockholm or Oslo, perhaps a legacy of its swashbuckling seafaring and trading history. Its gregarious English-speaking inhabitants can also seem positively welcoming compared with the icy reserve of their northerly neighbours.

If the city lacks anything you could say it's a true "blockbuster" attraction. Aside from the Little Mermaid and arguably the Tivoli Gardens, Copenhagen doesn't do the "queue round the block" tourism, while its most illustrious former inhabitants (Hans Christian Andersen aside) don't quite make the global pilgrimage hit list. Instead you'll discover a marvellously eclectic range of museums, galleries, designer shops and royal heritage buildings, all easily digestible and perfect for short-break perusing. For an idea of where to begin, turn to our itineraries and "where to" section.

Whether you're on foot, cycling (see box) or jumping on the user-friendly transport system you'll also find Copenhagen eminently navigable. You can quickly flit between neighbourhoods, from the cobbled avenues of Frederiksstaden and grand Slotsholmen island to the winding medieval streets of

Best places to explore on two wheels

Cycling is a way of life in Copenhagen – nearly everyone gets to school and work on two wheels. Pick up a snazzy bike for rent at Københavns Cyklebørs in Indre By, then pedal around Christianshavn's quiet canals, up to Kastellet to see the Little Mermaid or out to Frederiksberg's lush parks. Alternatively, hop on a train (bike in tow) up the coast, then pedal out to see the world-class art of the Louisiana Museum or around Kronborg Castle, one of the most handsome fortresses in the land.

When to visit

Easily Copenhagen's best season is summer, when both locals and visitors stay out nursing their drinks until the wee hours and cultural events such as the ten-day-long Copenhagen Jazz Festival bring live music, dance and art to the streets. Autumn and spring are similarly alluring – especially for cycling – since the afternoons remain warm but the majority of tourists have departed. Still, don't write off winter, a perfectly charming time for drinking *gløgg* (Scandinavian mulled wine) in cosy bars and enjoying the beloved Danish tradition of *hygge* (cosiness). The festive markets of Tivoli and Nyhavn and the Christmas lights make the city an excellent destination for a festive break.

the Latin Quarter and the gritty boho chic of Nørrebro. Green space and charming canals are never far away, whether in the landscaped Kongens Have, or postcard-cute Nyhavn. For those schooled in Dansk design and architecture a visit to Christianshavn will reveal the city's more adventurous side: big open skies and sleek glass and chrome modernism. Come nightfall and another Copenhagen emerges – Michelin-star chefs shout out orders, cocktails are shaken and craft beers cracked open (see opposite for the best neighbourhoods to try).

Given Denmark itself is small, the capital is nearby some other cracking destinations. Half an hour west is medieval Roskilde, home to a superb museum of Viking ships, one of Europe's biggest music festivals, and a museum of rock music, dubbed "the coolest museum in Demark". North of the capital, meanwhile, stands the outstanding modern art museum of Louisiana, the picture-perfect Renaissance castle of Kronborg and – across the iconic Øresund Bridge – the cool, diminutive Swedish city of Malmö, once part of Denmark's regal orbit.

Nyhavn

Where to...

Eating

At the time of writing the Danish capital boasted a record twenty-two Michelin stars – more than anywhere else in Scandinavia (see page 65). While advance booking at the better-known restaurants is recommended, Copenhagen isn't all haute cuisine: you can also find great local and international spots such as Christianshavn's *Bådudlejning*, *Ølhalle* and *Pintxos*, which will suit slimmer purses. Furthermore, restaurants all over the city often offer affordable lunchtime options, and you can always visit Nørrebro's Torvehallerne market for everything from organic wines to baked goods – especially on Sundays, when many restaurants close their doors anyway.
OUR FAVOURITES: Aamanns, see page 66. Amass see page 75. Relae, see page 95.

Drinking

Danes, apparently, drink more coffee than anywhere else in the world, and downtown Copenhagen is paradise for caffeine addicts – *Norden* café is one of Indre By's most popular. Many daytime cafés often morph into cosy and candlelit bars come evening time, and nearly anywhere in Copenhagen you can find music lilting from inside a chilled bar until late – perfect for enjoying a relaxing pint of Carlsberg or one of Denmark's many excellent microbrews (don't miss Ølfabrikken's traditional stouts). Most recently, the city has acquired some great wine bars, most notably in Vesterbro and Nørrebro.
OUR FAVOURITES: Coffee Collective, see page 64. Mikkeller, see page p.87.

Nightlife

If you're in the market for late nights out, the trendy meatpacking district of Kødbyen should be your first – or, rather, last – stop. This recently gentrified neighbourhood of lofts and warehouses has become one of Europe's hottest places to party with DJs, live bands and plenty of dancing. For something more mellow, try Sankt Hans Torv and the surrounding streets in Nørrebro, probably the best place in the city for a romantic late-night drink. Don't miss a shot of ice-cold caraway schnapps – a Danish speciality.
OUR FAVOURITES: Curfew, see page 86. Ruby, see page 43. Bo-Bi Bar, see page 42.

Shopping

To get your retail kicks, the central cobbled pedestrian Strøget offers large department stores, including Illums Bolighus, a favourite with the Danish queen, plus iconic local brands Royal Copenhagen and Georg Jensen. The nearby streets of Købmagergade and Kompagnistræde have small, independent holes-in-the-wall selling modern design objets and housewares, while the student-filled Latin Quarter is the place to head for secondhand fashion. South, Værnedamsvej in Vesterbro is great for local designers, while northerly Nørrebro (especially Elmegade and Blågårdsgade) offers chic shops with designers on hand to tailor the clothing on the racks.
OUR FAVOURITES: Royal Copenhagen, see page 37. Designer Zoo, see page 83. Paustian, see page 92.

Copenhagen at a glance

Nørrebro and Østerbro p.88.
Multicultural Nørrebro gentrified into the hipster epicentre, while the massive Fælledparken in leafy Østerbro is the city's most popular park.

Rosenborg and around p.60.
Gorge on art at Denmark's national gallery, then relax in the beautifully landscaped grounds of the Kongens Have (King's Garden).

Strøget and the Inner City p.30.
Hundreds of shops, dozens of cafés and a warren of medieval streets make the Inner City, or "Indre By", the beating heart of the city.

Vesterbro and Frederiksberg p.78.
Once grim and grimy, Vesterbro is now one of the city's hippest quarters – while tree-lined Frederiksberg is one of the most exclusive.

Tivoli and Rådhuspladsen p.24.
All the fun of the fair at Denmark's biggest and most elegant amusement park, plus Copenhagen's main civic square, fringed with refreshment stands.

Zoologisk Museum

Fælledp

Skateboardin Rink

TAGENSVEJ

NØRREBRO

NØRREBROGADE

Assistens Kirkegaard

Peblinge Sø

Musikmuseet (M)

Ørs pa

Sankt Jørgens Sø

Frederiksberg Rådhus

(M) (M)

FREDERIKSBERG

Frederiksberg Have

GAMMEL KONGEVEJ

(S)

T Gard

Zoologisk Have (Copenhagen Zoo)

Tycho Brahe Planetarium

(S)

Ce Sta

Frederiksberg Slot

VESTERBROGADE

Søndermarken

VESTERBRO

Elephant Gate

CARLSBERG DISTRICT

VALBY

(S)

LYNGBYVEJ

(S)

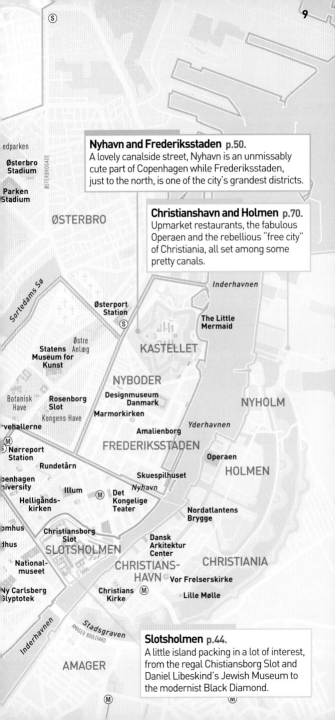

Nyhavn and Frederiksstaden p.50.
A lovely canalside street, Nyhavn is an unmissably cute part of Copenhagen while Frederiksstaden, just to the north, is one of the city's grandest districts.

Christianshavn and Holmen p.70.
Upmarket restaurants, the fabulous Operaen and the rebellious "free city" of Christiania, all set among some pretty canals.

Slotsholmen p.44.
A little island packing in a lot of interest, from the regal Chistiansborg Slot and Daniel Libeskind's Jewish Museum to the modernist Black Diamond.

edparken

Østerbro Stadium

Parken Stadium

ØSTERBRO

Sortedams Sø

Østerport Station

The Little Mermaid

Inderhavnen

Østre Anlæg

Statens Museum for Kunst

KASTELLET

Botanisk Have

Rosenborg Slot

Kongens Have

NYBODER

Designmuseum Danmark

Marmorkirken

NYHOLM

vehallerne

Nørreport Station

Amalienborg

Yderhavnen

FREDERIKSSTADEN

Rundetårn

Operaen

HOLMEN

openhagen niversity

Illum

Det Kongelige Teater

Skuespilhuset

Nyhavn

Helligånds- kirken

Nordatlantens Brygge

omhus

Christiansborg Slot

Dansk Arkitektur Center

hus

SLOTSHOLMEN

CHRISTIANIA

National- museet

CHRISTIANS- HAVN

Vor Frelserskirke

Ny Carlsberg Glyptotek

Christians Kirke

Lille Mølle

Inderhavnen

Stadsgraven

AMAGER BOULEVARD

AMAGER

ØSTERBROGADE

Inderhavnen

15

Things not to miss

It's not possible to see everything that Copenhagen has to offer in one trip – and we don't suggest you try. What follows is a selective taste of the city's highlights, from royal palaces to cutting-edge design.

> **Den Blå Planet**
See page 102
The Blue Planet is a jaw-dropping modern aquarium containing some 20,000 animals across 450 species.

< **Nationalmuseet**
See page 28
World-class collection of historical artefacts, from bog people and fifteenth-century BC sculptures to Viking weapons.

∨ **Nyhavn**
See page 50
This quaint, much-photographed, harbour is located just alongside a strip of popular bars and restaurants.

< Torvehallerne
See page 68

Beer from Mikkeller, Copenhagen's finest chocolate, and porridge reimagined as dinner are just some of the edible surprises at Denmark's largest food hall.

∨ Tivoli
See page 24

At this magical amusement park, one of the oldest in the world, you'll find hair-raising rides, enchanting gardens, and unforgettable live shows.

< Designmuseum Danmark
See page 54
Trace the evolution of Danish design, from Renaissance textiles to Arne Jacobsen chairs – Ikea it ain't.

∨ Zoologisk Have
See page 82
Founded in 1859, Copenhagen's zoo is home to 3,000 animals from 264 species. The stand-out sight is the Arctic polar bear habitat.

THINGS NOT TO MISS

∧ Rundetårn
See page 31
Instead of stairs, the oldest working observatory tower in Europe has a spectacular 209m spiral pathway.

< Nørrebro
See page 88
Once gritty, now gentrified by creative types, head here for Michelin-stars, superlative coffee, craft beer, and clusters of hip boutiques and vintage furniture shops.

∧ Statens Museum for Kunst
See page 61
Denmark's enormous art museum, with exceptional collections of Danish and international art from the last seven centuries.

∨ Den Sorte Diamant (The Black Diamond)
See page 49
This stunning, reflective piece of waterfront modernism is both a public library and a super spot for people-watching.

∧ Guards at Amalienborg
See page 51
Kids love the royal palace's poker-faced guards, who ceremoniously change their position every day at noon, with marching band accompaniment.

< Frederiksborg Slot
See page 99
Fairy-tale renaissance castle spread out across several small islands, featuring a lake, gardens, Gothic towers and spires.

< **Louisiana Museum of Modern Art**
See page 98
Denmark's most visited art gallery has a beachfront setting nearly as impressive as its collection.

∨ **Kødbyen**
See page 80
Copenhagen's meatpacking district is the hippest area for a night out.

Day One in Copenhagen

Latin Quarter, Inner City. See page 31. Begin the day strolling about this maze of lively medieval streets and squares around Copenhagen University, perfect for losing yourself in history.

Rådhus. See page 27. Climb to the tower of this grandiose, National Romantic city hall, whose fascinating astronomical clock is a destination in itself.

Lunch *Aamanns* (see page 66). This rustic-urban eatery does modern takes on the traditional Danish smørrebrød.

Canal Tour. See page 125. Join one of the multilingual hourly tours along Copenhagen's centuries-old canals, which offer fascinating insight into important events and sights tied to Denmark's tumultuous history.

Rosenborg Slot. See page 60. Explore your inner royal at this fairy-tale, red-brick Renaissance castle, whose cellar holds the Danish crown jewels and Frederik III's coronation throne, made of gold and narwhal tusk.

Nyboder. See page 65. Make your way out to the multicoloured terraced houses in this relaxed part of town, built in the seventeenth century to house the Danish navy.

Dinner *Toldboden* (see page 59). This spacious, casual restaurant is set opposite the royal yacht's mooring and is unbeatable for people-watching.

The Little Mermaid. See page 55. Stroll out to Kastellet to catch a glimpse of Copenhagen's mascot and the heroine of Hans Christian Andersen's fairy tale.

Rosenborg Slot

Yellow houses in Nyboder district

Toldboden

Day Two in Copenhagen

Ny Carlsberg Glyptotek. See page 26. Start off in this brilliant museum, which holds a vast classical and modern European art collection displayed in opulent rooms.

Krigsmuseet. See page 47. Exhibitions on current and past war battles, including hundreds of Danish military ships from seventeenth century and the 156m arched hall housing the cannon collection.

Christiania. See page 71. Amble along the pretty Christianshavns Kanal, designed by an Amsterdam-born architect, before exploring this renowned hippie "free city" commune.

Lunch *Cofoco* (see page 84). Enjoy a variety of scrumptious "Nordic tapas" from a long and seasonally changing menu at this popular spot.

Frederiksberg Have. See page 81. Pedal out towards Værnedamsvej for a spot of fashionista window shopping, then put down on the open expanses of grass at the city's most wild parklands.

Musikmuseet. See page 79. Giraffe pianos are just some of the unusual instruments on display at the Music Museum, which reopened in DR's former Radio House in 2014.

Helsingør. See page 101. Ride the train up the coast to watch the sun set against Kronborg, a fairy-tale fortress and the inspiration for Elsinore Castle in Shakespeare's *Hamlet*.

Dinner *Brasserie Nimb* (see page 29). Great traditional French food with a regularly changing menu in an Oriental-style palace, located on the edge of the Tivoli Gardens.

Ny Carlsberg Glyptotek

Christiania

Helsingør

Kids' Copenhagen

Families will find plenty to keep the kids happy, from amusement parks to swimming pools, science museums to playgrounds.

Tivoli. See page 24. This magical fairground has roller coasters, pantomime theatres and endless helpings of family fun.

Havneparken. See page 74. Combine shopping with swimming at Fisketorvet's Copencabana, popular with children thanks to its two outdoor pools and diving boards built right into the harbour.

Rundetårn. See page 31. This 42m-high stone church tower has an observatory at the top offering great vistas across to the city's numerous spires.

Harbour Bath Fisketorvet

🍴 **Lunch** *Det Lille Apotek* (see page 39). Oldest restaurant in the city with leadlight windows and oil lamps; a great atmosphere for sampling some typical Danish dishes.

Ridebane. See page 45. Visit the Royal Stables, whose regal, marble-clad stables are home to golden carriages and beautiful horses.

Experimentarium. See page 91. This huge science lab lets kids learn about the human body, physics and the natural world, all with hands-on high-energy exhibits.

Training horses at Royal Stables

🍴 **Dinner** *Madklubben* (see pages 57 and 85). This much-loved Danish chain offers delicious meals at surprisingly affordable prices.

Experimentarium

Budget Copenhagen

Though Copenhagen is one of Europe's most expensive cities, you can save cash by using a discount card, riding free city bikes, taking harbour bus-boats and visiting many of the city's free-entry museums.

National Museum. See page 28. Home to Denmark's finest ethnographic artefacts, including an extensive collection of Viking weapons and coins.

Amalienborg. See page 51. A few metres from the harbourfront, soldiers participate in the Changing of the Guard here at noon every day.

Lunch Pick up some bread, cheese and drinks, then picnic on the grass of Kongens Have (see page 61), the city's most popular green space.

Amalienborg

Marmorkirken. See page 53. This marble church was built in 1894 in the image of St Peter's in Rome; join the 1pm tour to ascend the 260 steps to the dome's apogee for some grand city views.

Slotsholmen. See page 44. Descend a narrow stairwell to explore the ruins of two excavated underground castles.

Assistens Kirkegaard. See page 89. Cross the western lakes to take in the final resting place of Danish luminaries such as Hans Christian Andersen and Niels Bohr.

Galerie Asbæk. See page 56. This much-loved gallery represents some of Denmark's best-known painters and photographers and is great for a spot of window shopping.

The impressive Marble Church

Dinner *Vespa* (see page 59). This simple, down-at-heel Italian restaurant's four-course set menus are outstanding value for money.

Kongens Have

PLACES

Tivoli and Rådhuspladsen......................**24**

Strøget and the Inner City **30**

Slotsholmen..**44**

Nyhavn and Frederiksstaden.................**50**

Rosenborg and around...........................**60**

Christianshavn and Holmen **70**

Vesterbro and Frederiksberg **78**

Nørrebro and Østerbro **88**

Day-trips...**98**

Malmö..**106**

Copenhagen is one of the most bicycle-friendly cities in the world

Tivoli and Rådhuspladsen

Tivoli, Denmark's most-visited attraction, may appear at first glance every bit as tacky as any other amusement park around the world, but it has much more to offer than just its thrilling set of rides. After taking in the 83,000-square-metre gardens, with their gorgeous flower displays and fountains, romantic boating lake, exotic-looking buildings (from Chinese pagodas to Moorish palaces) and – at night – spectacular illuminations, even the most cynical visitor will have to succumb and agree that it's a magical (albeit expensive) place. A few paces away is the buzzing Rådhuspladsen square, towered over by the grand red-brick nineteenth-century city hall, whose innards hold a fascinating astronomical clock. As well as demarcating the city's geographical heart, the square is the perfect place for a mustard-topped *pølse*.

Tivoli

MAP P.25, POCKET MAP A13
Vesterbrogade 3 ① 33 15 10 01, ⑩ tivoli. dk. April 4 to Sept 22, three weeks in Oct & mid-Nov to Jan 5 Mon–Thurs & Sun 11am–11pm, Fri & Sat 11am–midnight. Adults and children aged 8 and over 130kr; under-8s 60kr, Tivoli card grants free access for children, multi-ride pass 240kr.

Tivoli

Opened in 1843, **Tivoli** was the creation of architect George Carstensen, who had been commissioned by Christian VIII to build a pleasure garden for the masses outside the western gate into the city. It was an immediate success, and – expanded and modernized over the years – was a major influence on Walt Disney for his theme parks a century later. That the gardens continue even today to occupy such a patch of prime real estate, sandwiched between the Hovedbanegården and the Rådhus, is testimony to Tivoli's central place within the city's affections.

Tivoli's principal draw, of course – to children at least – is its twenty-five-odd **rides**, which include one of the world's oldest still-functioning wooden roller coasters. Still more hair-raising are the Star Flyer, which lifts up and twirls thrill-seekers around some 80m above ground, and Aquila, which thrusts its victims around at the nauseating force of 4G. Music, theatre and panto (mostly free once you're in) are a key part of Tivoli's

What lies beneath: digging up the town

The opening of the new orbital metro in late 2019 involved large parts of the old city being excavated, the most extensive building work since Christian IV (aka the builder king) erected most of Copenhagen's defensive works, castles and churches in the sixteenth century.
Archeologists from the Københavns Museum (closed at the time of writing while it is relocated) are having a field day (literally) unlocking the city's underground secrets before the diggers are let loose, and some aspects of its history are now under revision. Data emerged indicating, for example, that a major settlement existed here before Bishop Absalon founded Copenhagen in the twelfth century and that the settlers at the time were much taller than previously thought.
The WALL, an interactive mobile twelve-metre screen, follows the excavators around, providing above-ground news on the latest finds and discoveries underneath. For information on where to find it, consult Ⓦ m.dk and Ⓦ copenhagen.dk.

appeal, with over five stages and several bandstands. Pantomime – in the classic Italian *commedia dell'arte* tradition – is put on throughout the year in the extraordinary

Chinese-style **Pantomime Theatre**, and every Friday evening in season at 10pm there's a hugely popular gig (Ⓦ fredagsrock.dk) at the open-air **Plænen** stage, featuring mainly

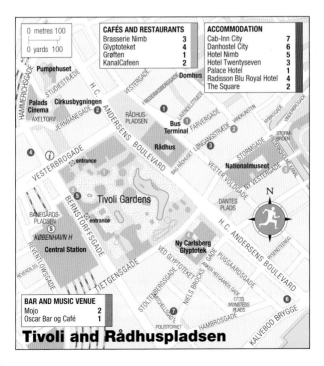

Tivoli and Rådhuspladsen

Ny Carlsberg Glyptotek

Scandinavian acts. The gardens can get crowded but the setting is magical and the atmosphere buzzing – and Tivoli's undulating layout means that you can always find a peaceful and picturesque nook from which to relax and drink in the scene.

Formerly only open during summertime, in recent years Tivoli has extended its season to include three weeks leading up to **Halloween**, when the gardens are bestrewn with smiley pumpkins and clingy cobwebs, and a six-week **Christmas market**, when the best of Danish Yuletide traditions are on show.

Central Station

MAP P.25, POCKET MAP A14
Designed by station builder extraordinaire Heinrich Wenck as a *Gesamtkunstwerk* (total work of art), the hulking yet elegant **Hovedbanegården** (Central Station) is one of the country's most noteworthy National Romantic buildings. Dating from 1911, it's built predominantly in red brick, slate and granite, as dictated by the style, with abundant decorative detail – all of which Wenck was responsible for. Note in particular the large wood-beamed (rather than cast-iron) arches supporting the roof structure above the central hall and platforms, and the magnificent chandeliers.

The station is home to the studio of a national television channel, TV2. Journalists from the daily *Go'morgen Danmark* ("Good Morning Denmark") breakfast show often canvass opinions on the issues of the day from passing travellers, so don't be surprised if you're suddenly stopped for a quick interview.

Ny Carlsberg Glyptotek

MAP P.25, POCKET MAP B14
Dantes Plads 7 ☎ 33 41 81 41,
🌐 glyptoteket.dk.dk. Tues, Wed & Fri-Sun 11am–6pm, Thurs 11am–9pm; 115kr, free on Tues. Free guided tours in English mid-

June to mid-Sept noon & 1pm (rest of the
year in Danish only).

Impossible to miss with its opulent
red-brick Venetian Renaissance
facade, the exquisite **Ny Carlsberg
Glyptotek** was established by
brewing magnate Carl Jacobsen
(1842–1914) to provide a public
home for his vast private art
collection. The building and
collection have since been extended
and expanded several times, the
gallery's richly decorated rooms
providing as captivating a spectacle
as the remarkable haul of ancient
and modern works on display.

The main entrance takes you into
the museum's original building
(1897), designed by Danish
architect **Vilhelm Dahlerup**.
Housed within its two floors of
extravagantly colourful friezes,
marble pillars and mosaic floors are
sculptures and paintings from the
Danish Golden Age, including
Bertel Thorvaldsen's evocative
The Three Graces relief, and a fine
collection of **French sculpture**,
with particular emphasis on Rodin
– the largest collection of his work
outside France. The undoubted
highlight of the Dahlerup section,
however, is the tranquil, glass-
domed **Winter Garden** around
which it centres, filled with palm
trees, statues and a fountain. The
museum café here serves arguably
Scandinavia's best cake (see
page 29).

On the opposite side of the
Winter Garden, the large marble-
pillared Central Hall of the
elaborate **Kampmann** extension
(1905) leads to an extensive
Ancient Mediterranean collection,
which starts around 6000 BC
and traces the development of
the Greek, Etruscan and Roman
empires. From the Central Hall
a set of stairs leads up to a newer
wing designed by Henning Larsen
(of the Opera House; see page
74), a courtyard infill housing a
fantastic collection of **French post-
impressionist** paintings including
noteworthy pieces by Degas, Manet
and Gauguin.

The Rådhus

MAP P.25, POCKET MAP B13
Rådhuspladsen ☎ 33 66 33 66. Mon–Fri
9am–4pm, Sat 1am–1pm. Access to Jens
Olsen's World Clock 10kr. Tower Mon–Fri
11am & 2pm, Sat noon; 40kr; Tours in
English Mon–Fri 1pm, Sat 10am, 50kr.

Dominating Rådhuspladsen, the
city's bustling cobbled main square
(much of it currently cordoned
off by metro building works), is
the grand **Rådhus** (City Hall)
from 1905, a great example of
the National Romantic style with
beautiful and intricate decorative
detail throughout. Just past the

Axeltorv Square: circus friezes and multicoloured facades

Vesterport, once the western gate into the city, has some notable
architectural landmarks. Cirkusbygningen ("the Circus Building")
was built in the 1880s; note the elaborate horse-racing frieze that
still encircles the building. Now a venue for dinner shows, in its
heyday the adjoining stables stretched as far as Studiestræde
and housed circus horses, giraffes and elephants. On the other
side of Axeltorv, 17-screen Palads cinema opened in 1912, its
brightly coloured facade added in 1989 by Danish abstract artist
Poul Gerners. The building site opposite is the ghost of the Scala
entertainment complex, which despite its popularity in the 1990s
was torn down in 2012; five grandly designed, landmark office
towers are envisioned in its place.

entrance, the stately main hall has walls of layered polished red brick and limestone (a reference to the national flag) and an impressive arched gallery, beneath which a limestone strip is inscribed with key moments in Copenhagen's history. As a working public building the City Hall is open to visitors, though the informative **tours** are the best way to capture its full detail. Tours include access to the 105m **tower**, which gives stunning views of the city, and **Jens Olsen's world clock** – an extraordinary astronomical timepiece from 1955 with hundreds of ticking dials tracking the planetary movement with astounding accuracy.

Nationalmuseet

MAP P.25, POCKET MAP C13
Ny Vestergade 10 ☎ 33 13 44 11,
Ⓦ natmus.dk. Tues–Sun 10am–5pm. Free.
Housed in an eighteenth-century Rococo palace, formerly the Danish Crown Prince's residence, the immense **National Museum**'s vast collection, which stretches from prehistory to the present day via the Viking period and Middle Ages, could easily take days to go

through. If you're short of time, head straight for the second floor and the captivating **Inuit** part of the vast **Ethnographic** collection, the most extensive of its kind in the world. There's a wealth of detail on their hunting techniques and exhibits include dog sledges and some amazing hand-carved kayaks. It also provides a succinct account of the events leading to Denmark's colonization of Greenland.

Standout among the exhibits in the **Danish prehistory** section are the magical gold-plated Trundholm Sun Chariot, dating from around 1400 BC, which has featured on many a Danish stamp since its discovery in 1902, and – above all – the bog-preserved **Egtved Girl** (1370 BC), who still has her clothes, hair and jewellery intact. Finally, a detour to the **Viking exhibition** will categorically banish the perception that all Vikings did was rape and pillage. Room 23 gives an insight into the remarkable distances they travelled – as far as present-day Iran and Afghanistan – on their trade and diplomatic missions to gather silver, the main currency of the era.

Nationalmuseet

Cafés and restaurants

Brasserie Nimb

MAP P.25, POCKET MAP A13
Bernstorffsgade 5 ⓘ 88 70 00 10, ⓦ nimb.dk.
One of four restaurants within
the lavish *Nimb Hotel*, Tivoli's
romantic fairy-tale *Arabian Nights*-
style palace (though also accessible
from outside the gardens), the
ground-floor *Brasserie* is a temple
to traditional French cuisine. Open
throughout the year.

Glyptoteket

MAP P.25, POCKET MAP B14
Dantes Plads 7 ⓘ 33 41 81 41,
ⓦ glyptoteket.dk. Tues–Sun 11am–6pm.
Even if the Ny Carlsberg
Glyptotek's art and sculpture don't
grab you, it's worth visiting the
café, occupying a beautiful position
in the glass-domed Winter Garden,
for exquisite smørrebrød (from
119kr) and cake (from 45kr).

Grøften

Grøften

MAP P.25, POCKET MAP A13
Tivoli ⓘ 33 75 06 75, ⓦ groeften.dk. Sun–
Thurs 12am–10pm, Fri–Sat 12am–11pm.
Historic restaurant with seating
outdoors on a large open terrace,
popular with celebs of a certain
vintage. The overloaded prawn
sandwich (129kr) and the all-you-
can-eat *skipperlabskovs* (Danish
goulash; 165kr) are legendary, as is
the smørrebrød (from 79kr).

KanalCafeen

MAP P.25, POCKET MAP C13
Frederiksholms Kanal 18 ⓘ 33 11 57 70,
ⓦ kanalcafeen.dk. Mon–Fri 11.30am–5pm,
Sat 11.30am–3pm.
Founded in 1852, this cosy, historic
lunchtime restaurant opposite
Christiansborg serves outstanding,
good-value smørrebrød (from 66kr
for marinated herring). Inside, the
decor is all heavy tablecloths and
period oil paintings, while outside
there's canal side seating in summer.

Bar

Oscar Bar og Café

MAP P.25, POCKET MAP B13
Rådhuspladsen 77 ⓘ 33 12 09 99,
ⓦ oscarbarcafe.dk. Sun–Thurs
11am–11pm, Fri & Sat 11am–2am.
Set just next to the Rådhus, this
very popular gay bar is lively and
well lit, and has DJs pumping tunes
out until late on weekends. Happy
hour (5–9pm) has 34kr Carlsbergs,
and there are good sandwiches and
burgers (from 99kr) too.

Music venue

Mojo

MAP P.25, POCKET MAP C13
Løngangstræde 21C ⓘ 33 11 64 53,
ⓦ mojo.dk. Daily 8pm–5am.
This authentic, smoky bar with
sticky beer-stained tables is a must
for blues aficionados. The live gigs
(most nights from 9.30pm) are
usually free, though chargeable
(up to 150kr) when bigger names
are playing.

Strøget and the Inner City

Indre By ("inner city") is Copenhagen's heart and hub, its compact warren of narrow streets and cobbled squares home to the capital's principal shopping district and countless bars and restaurants. For centuries Indre By was Copenhagen, springing into life with the arrival of Bishop Absalon in 1167, and fortified with stone walls until the nineteenth century. Historic buildings rub shoulders with modern but the area, bisected by the bustling pedestrianized thoroughfare of Strøget, is at its most atmospheric around the Latin Quarter, original home to the university, and pretty, colourful Gråbrødre Torv.

Strøget

MAP P.32, POCKET MAP B12–D11

The principal artery of the city's main shopping district, **Strøget** is a series of five interconnecting pedestrian streets, over 1km in length, which runs from Rådhuspladsen to Kongens Nytorv (see page 34). One of the world's first pedestrian strips when it was created in 1962, it's abuzz with life 24/7 from the constant flow of shoppers during the day and revellers at night. Street entertainers and fruit and snack sellers also ply their trade – the weeks before Christmas are especially lively, with carol singers, shoppers galore and delicious treats – such as *æbleskiver* (sweet, deep-fried apple dumplings) and *gløgg* (mulled wine) on sale.

Amagertorv

The Rådhuspladsen end of Strøget, beginning with **Frederiksberggade**, is fairly tacky but the strip gradually goes more upmarket, running past some of the city's oldest buildings and squares. On **Gammeltorv** (Old Square), look out for the **Caritas Fountain**, which predates the (much more famous) Manneken Pis in Brussels, and features a woman spraying water from her breasts as a small boy pees into the basin.

From here, Strøget continues past Amagertorv (see page 33), culminating in a line of exclusive designer stores as it reaches Østergade and Kongens Nytorv (see page 34).

Rundetårn

MAP P.32, POCKET MAP C11
Købmagergade 52A ☎ 33 73 03 73,
ⓦ rundetaarn.dk. Tower: April–Sept,
10am–8pm; October–March, Thurs–Mon
10am–6pm, Tues–Wed 10am–9pm.
Observatory: 6pm–9pm. 25kr.

Built by Christian IV in the mid-seventeenth century, the 42m-high **Rundetårn** (Round Tower) originally formed part of a larger complex, functioning both as church tower and **observatory**. The observatory, at the top of the tower, is still operational – the oldest of its kind still in use in Europe – and can be visited in wintertime, while the ascent, along a wide, cobbled walkway, is straightforward even for vertigo sufferers. As you make your way up, you can catch your breath at the **modern art gallery** in the former university library hall, and at the various other quirky exhibits en route, including Christian IV's toilet. The view from the top, across the city's many towers and spires, is fabulous.

The Latin Quarter

MAP P.32, POCKET MAP B11
Frue Plads.

In one of the city's most historic areas, the buildings of the so-called

Rundetårn

Latin Quarter around Fiolstræde date back to the foundation of Scandinavia's earliest university in 1475. Hailing from 1836, the grand neo-Gothic **university** building across Frue Plads from Vor Frue Kirke serves a primarily administrative purpose today – most of the university departments have relocated outside the city centre. On one side a row of busts of the university's rationalist scholars – including Nobel prize-winning Niels Bohr – faces off against busts of religious men lining the cathedral wall opposite.

Helligåndskirken

MAP P.32, POCKET MAP C12
Amagertorv. ⓦ helligaandskirken.dk.
Mon–Fri noon–4pm, Sat 11am–1pm (plus services on Sun).

One of the city's oldest churches, dating back to the thirteenth century, the **Helligåndskirken** (Church of the Holy Ghost) was originally part of a Catholic monastery. Following

Vor Frue Kirke

Helligåndshuset, survives in the church's west wing (to the left of the entrance) as the city's largest and most intact medieval building. It's not hard to imagine its past incarnation as a medieval hospital, beds crammed in between the slender granite columns that hold up the heavy vaulted ceiling. Today it houses regular flea markets, concerts and exhibitions.

Vor Frue Kirke

MAP P.32, POCKET MAP B11
Frue Plads ☎ 33 15 10 78,
ⓦ koebenhavnsdomkirke.dk. Daily 8am–5pm, except during services.
The plain, rather sombre-looking **Vor Frue Kirke** (Church of Our Lady) dates from 1829 and has functioned as Copenhagen's cathedral since 1923, though there's been a church on this site since the eleventh century. It's not until you're through the

the Reformation it became a Lutheran church, and although repeatedly destroyed (by fire and bombardment), an evocative section of the monastery, the

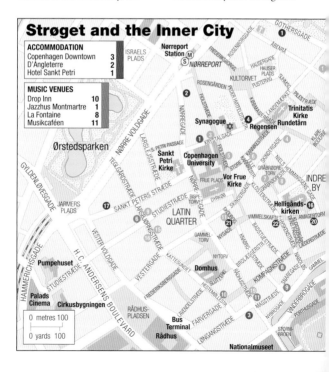

Strøget and the Inner City

ACCOMMODATION
Copenhagen Downtown	3
D'Angleterre	2
Hotel Sankt Petri	1

MUSIC VENUES
Drop Inn	10
Jazzhus Montmartre	1
La Fontaine	8
Musikcaféen	11

0 metres 100
0 yards 100

heavy Doric-pillared portal into the whitewashed Neoclassical interior that its more elegant features are revealed. A simple carved frieze above the altar accentuates a magnificent statue of Christ by Bertel Thorvaldsen (see page 47); the statue's hand positioning gave Thorvaldsen much grief before he finally decided on the open downward-facing position appreciated by both Catholics and Protestants alike. In 2004, the cathedral briefly hit the international spotlight as the venue for the wedding of Crown Prince Frederik and his Tasmanian wife Mary.

Amagertorv and Højbro Plads

MAP P.32, POCKET MAP C12–D12

If Strøget has a focal point, it's the L-shaped interconnecting squares of **Amagertorv** and **Højbro Plads**. On the direct route

between the once royal residence of Christiansborg and Vor Frue Kirke these two squares have borne witness to numerous coronation parties, royal weddings and (prior to the Reformation) religious processions. They're especially bustling in summertime when the cafés set up outside and snack vendors and bicycle-rickshaw operators ply their trade. Tourists seem perpetually drawn to pose by the two artworks by sculptor Vilhem Bissen: an equestrian statue of Bishop Absalon and the *Storkespringvandet* (Stork Fountain), while a more recent addition is the beautiful mosaic paving by Bjørn Nørgaard (see page 45).

Købmagergade and around

MAP P.32, POCKET MAP D11

On the corner of Strøget and the busy pedestrianized side street

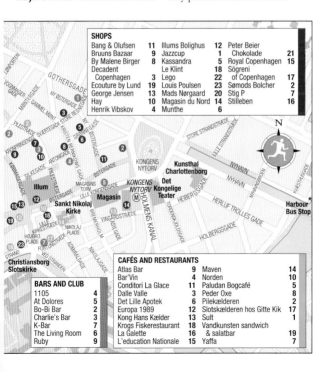

SHOPS

Bang & Olufsen	11	Illums Bolighus	12	Peter Beier		
Bruuns Bazaar	9	Jazzcup	1	Chokolade	21	
By Malene Birger	8	Kassandra	5	Royal Copenhagen	15	
Decadent		Le Klint	18	Søgreni		
Copenhagen	3	Lego	22	of Copenhagen	17	
Ecouture by Lund	19	Louis Poulsen	23	Sømods Bolcher	2	
George Jensen	13	Mads Nørgaard	20	Stig P	7	
Hay	10	Magasin du Nord	14	Stilleben	16	
Henrik Vibskov	4	Munthe	6			

CAFÉS AND RESTAURANTS

Atlas Bar	9	Maven	14
Bar'Vin	4	Norden	10
Conditori La Glace	11	Paludan Bogcafé	5
Dalle Valle	3	Peder Oxe	8
Det Lille Apotek	6	Pilekælderen	2
Europa 1989	12	Slotskælderen hos Gitte Kik	17
Kong Hans Kælder	13	Sult	1
Krogs Fiskerestaurant	18	Vandkunsten sandwich	
La Galette	16	& salatbar	19
L'education Nationale	15	Yaffa	7

BARS AND CLUB

1105	4
At Dolores	5
Bo-Bi Bar	2
Charlie's Bar	3
K-Bar	7
The Living Room	6
Ruby	9

of **Købmagergade**, the Illum department store is one of the city's top places to shop, full of labels including Acne and Paul Smith. Running off Købmagergade to the east is a super-trendy knot of lanes – most notably **Pilestræde** – littered with exclusive designer shops.

Kongens Nytorv

MAP P.32, POCKET MAP E11

The city's grandest square, **Kongens Nytorv** was for years the main entrance to the royal part of the city. The "King's New Square" was laid out in 1670 by Christian V as part of a large urban expansion project. A 1688-era bronze statue of him thus stands at its centre – the oldest equestrian statue in Scandinavia, in fact. You'll also come across a copper-clad Baroque telephone kiosk from 1913.

The Royal Danish Theatre

Det Kongelige Teater

MAP P.32, POCKET MAP E11
Kongens Nytorv ⓣ 33 69 69 33,
ⓦ kglteater.dk. Tours roughly every other Sun 11am.

Somewhat confusingly, **Det Kongelige Teater** (the Royal Theatre) comprises three buildings: the main building on Kongens Nytorv, the Opera House on Holmen (see page 74) and the Skuespilhuset (see page 53). Built in 1874, the Kongens Nytorv theatre is by far the oldest of the three, and for years was the country's main national performance venue, hosting opera, ballet and drama under one roof – though today it is primarily used for ballet. As a fourteen-year-old, Hans Christian Andersen is known to have tried his luck as a ballet dancer here though the audition was, by all accounts, a disaster. To fully experience the theatre's grandeur you'll have to watch a performance.

Shops

Bang & Olufsen

MAP P.32, POCKET MAP D11
Østergade 18 ☎ 33 11 14 15, 🌐 bang-
olufsen.com. Mon–Fri 10am–6pm, Sat
10am–4pm.
At B&O's sleek flagship store you
can check out their latest top-of-
the-range sound and vision kit:
good to look at even if it might
stretch beyond your holiday
budget. Attention to detail and
built with high quality materials,
B&O's wide variety of headphones
will satisfy any customer willing to
open their wallet.

Bruuns Bazaar

MAP P.32, POCKET MAP C11
Kronprinsensgade 8–9 ☎ 33 32 19 99,
🌐 bruunsbazaar.dk. Mon–Thurs 10am–
6pm, Fri 10am–7pm, Sat 11am–4pm.
Two minimalist neighbouring
stores selling simple, stylish and
beautifully made clothes – ladies'
at no. 8, gents' at no. 9 – created
by in-house designers, hence the
somewhat hefty price tag.

By Malene Birger

MAP P.32, POCKET MAP D11
Antonigade 10 ☎ 35 43 22 33
🌐 bymalenebirger.com. Mon–Thurs
10am–6pm, Fri 10am–7pm, Sat 10am–5pm.
International designer store. You
can rent a look for a day, if you
don't want to spend over 2999kr
for a simple dress.

Decadent Copenhagen

MAP P.32, POCKET MAP D11
Store Regnegade 3 ☎ 70 70 36 37,
🌐 decadentcopenhagen.com. Mon–Fri
11am–5.30pm, Sat 11am–4pm.
Flagship store of this Danish
line, which began making high-
quality, trendy yet practical leather
women's handbags, and has since
branched out into shoes. Bags start
around 2000kr.

Ecouture by Lund

MAP P.32, POCKET MAP C12

Hay

Læderstræde 5 ☎ 27 58 57 30, 🌐 ecouture.
dk. Wed 12–5.30pm, Fri 12–6.30pm, Sat
noon–4pm.
You can now find the glamorous,
bohemian women's clothing line
with organic/socially responsible
stance (hence the "eco" in the name)
in a central location – although
opening hours remain restricted.

George Jensen

MAP P.32, POCKET MAP D12
Amagertorv 4 ☎ 33 11 40 80,
🌐 georgejensen.com. Mon–Sat 10am–6pm.
Silverware designed in the
spirit and style of the celebrated
silversmith Georg Jensen, who
first became known for his Art
Nouveau-style jewellery in the early
twentieth century. A small museum
inside tells his story.

Hay

MAP P.32, POCKET MAP D11
Pilestræde 29–31 ☎ 42 82 08 20, 🌐 hay.dk.
Mon–Fri 10am–6pm, Sat 10am–5pm.
Colourful, funky household
accessories, including furniture
and rugs, mostly by cutting-edge
Danish designers. A stunning
modular sofa in grey wool will cost
you 16,000kr.

Illums Bolighus

Henrik Vibskov

MAP P.32, POCKET MAP C11
Krystalgade 6 ☎ 33 14 61 00,
🌐 henrikvibskovboutique.com. Mon–Thurs
11am–6pm, Fri 11am–7pm, Sat 11am–5pm.
Weird and wonderful (and pricey)
gear from Copenhagen's *enfant
terrible* clothes designer. Henrik,
also an artist and drummer,
is notorious for his colourful,
flamboyant and über-trendy men's
and women's wear.

Illums Bolighus

MAP P.32, POCKET MAP D12
Amagertorv 10 ☎ 33 14 19 41,
🌐 illumsbolighus.dk. Mon–Thurs
10am–7pm, Fri 10am–8pm, Sat 10am–7pm,
Sun 11am–5pm.
A Copenhagen institution, this
gorgeous design department store
sells everything from top-of-
the-range clothes to furniture
and kitchenware from global
designer icons. It's also the place
to go year-round for beautiful
Christmas decorations.

Jazzcup

MAP P.32, POCKET MAP C10
Gothersgade 107 ☎ 33 33 87 40,
🌐 jazzklubben.dk. Tues–Thurs 10am–

5.30pm, Fri 10am–6pm, Sat 10am–2pm.
Excellent music store specializing in
jazz, blues, soul and world music.
It also has a small café and hosts
regular, intimate live shows (Fri
3.30pm, Sat 2.30pm).

Kassandra

MAP P.32, POCKET MAP D11
Grønnegade 27 ☎ 33 91 08 89. Mon–Fri
11am–6pm, Sat 11am–3pm.
One of the most beloved shoe
stores in the city, with scores of
the latest heels from highbrow
labels that include Jimmy Choo,
Stella McCartney, Chloé and Pedro
Garcia. Kassandra also sells bags
from the same designers.

Le Klint

MAP P.32, POCKET MAP D12
Store Kirkestræde 1 ☎ 33 11 66 63,
🌐 leklint.com. Tues–Fri 10am–6pm, Sat
10am–4pm.
Originally started by famous
furniture designer Kaare Klint, Le
Klint's lamps are now a globally
sought-after brand. The current
in-house designers have maintained
his simple, aesthetic style.

Lego

MAP P.32, POCKET MAP C12
Vimmelskaftet 37 🌐 stores.lego.com. Mon–
Thurs & Sat 10am–6pm, Fri 10am–7pm,
Sun 11am–5pm.
A must for Lego connoisseurs of
all ages, the flagship store even
provides building tips and tricks,
and can get you replacement pieces
for those crucial ones you've lost
from the colourful and never-
ending Pick-a-Brick wall.

Louis Poulsen

MAP P.32, POCKET MAP D12
Gammel Strand 28 ☎ 70 33 14 14,
🌐 louispoulsen.com. Mon–Fri 8am–5pm.
Beautiful lighting from top
designers past and present
including Poul Henningsen whose
famous glare-free PH lamps, made
up of concentric circular metal
shades, were launched in this store
many moons ago.

Mads Nørgaard

MAP P.32, POCKET MAP C12
Amagertorv 13–15 ☎ **33 32 01 28,**
🌐 **madsnorgaard.com. Mon–Thurs**
10am–6pm, Fri 10am–7pm, Sat 10am–5pm.
Good-quality, own-design
everyday wear for women and
children (at no. 13) and men
(no. 15) in cheerful, often stripy
colours. Prices are reasonable for
what you get.

Magasin du Nord

MAP P.32, POCKET MAP E12
Kongens Nytorv 13 ☎ **33 11 44 33,**
🌐 **magasin.dk. Daily 10am–8pm.**
This age-old department store is
still going strong, selling top-notch
clothes and homeware. Head to
the basement for the gourmet food
hall, well stocked with organic and
fair-trade foodstuffs and wines.
You'll also find magazines and
newspapers from around the globe
down here.

Munthe

MAP P.32, POCKET MAP D11
Grønnegade 10 ☎ **33 32 00 12,** 🌐 **dk.**
munthe.com. Mon–Fri 10am–6pm, Sat
10am–4pm.
Pricey and exciting – bordering
on grungy – women's clothing,
designed by Naja Munthe. Known
for its exquisite details, feminine
lines and high-quality materials, the
collection is completely renewed
every three months.

Peter Beier Chokolade

MAP P.32, POCKET MAP B12
Skoubogade 1 ☎ **33 93 07 17,**
🌐 **pbchokolade.dk. Mon–Thurs 10am–6pm,**
Fri 10am–7pm, Sat 10am–5pm.
Wonderful selection of handmade
chocolates, made with the finest
ingredients. The cocoa comes
from their own plantation in the
Caribbean.

Royal Copenhagen

MAP P.32, POCKET MAP C12
Amagertorv 6 ☎ **33 13 71 81,**
🌐 **royalcopenhagen.com. Mon–Fri 10am–**
7pm, Sat 10am–6pm, Sun 11am–4pm.
Flagship store for the Royal
Porcelain Factory's famous
china, distinguished by its blue
patterning. The beautiful gabled
store building, from 1616, is one
of the city's oldest, having survived
countless city-centre fires. Prices
start at 249kr for a decorated
egg cup.

Sögreni of Copenhagen

MAP P.32, POCKET MAP A12
Sankt Peders Stræde 30A ☎ **33 12 78 79,**
🌐 **sogrenibikes.com. Mon–Sun 10am–6pm.**
Sögreni's beautiful handmade bikes
are assembled in store, though with
prices starting at around 12,000kr
they don't come cheap. It's a
great place to come and buy bike
accessories, such as chain guards
and lights, which are also designed
and crafted in-house. Items begin
at around 290kr for a pretty little
copper bike bell.

Peter Beier Chokolade

Sømods Bolcher

MAP P.32, POCKET MAP B11
Nørregade 36 ☎ 33 12 60 46, ⓦ soemods-
bolcher.dk. Mon–Thurs 9.15am–5.30pm,
Fri 9.15am–6pm, Sat 10am–3.30pm, Sun
11am–3pm.

Dinky little confectioner that uses
age-old methods – dating back
to its establishment in 1891 – to
produce beautiful boiled and hand-
rolled candy in myriad colours
and flavours.

Stig P

MAP P.32, POCKET MAP D11
Kronprinsensgade 14 ☎ 33 14 42 16,
ⓦ stig-p.com. Mon–Fri 11am–6pm, Sat
10am–4pm.

This colourful, welcoming women's
clothes store was the first to open
on trendy Kronprinsensgade,
way back in 1969. Designer wear
encompasses Stella McCartney,
Calvin Klein and Stig P's own label.

Stilleben

MAP P.32, POCKET MAP C12
Niels Hemmingsensgade 3 ☎ 33 91 11 31,
ⓦ stilleben.dk. Mon–Fri 10am–6pm, Sat
10am–4pm.

Funky ceramics, glass, textiles and
much, much more from mostly

Stilleben

Danish designers. They seem to
specialize in quirky items that,
once seen, you'll never be able to
live without.

Cafés and restaurants

Atlas Bar

MAP P.32, POCKET MAP B12
Larsbjørnsstræde 18 ☎ 33 15 03 52,
ⓦ atlasbar.dk. Mon–Sat noon–10pm.

Informal café-cum-restaurant
serving affordable dishes from
around the globe in a charming,
laidback setting. There is an
extensive vegetarian menu
(including delicious nut burgers
made with hazelnuts, carrots and
celeriac; 135kr/195kr for lunch/
dinner) with a good range of freshly
made salads, and lots of freshly
squeezed juices, too.

Bar'Vin

MAP P.32, POCKET MAP C11
Skindergade 3 ☎ 33 12 58 03, ⓦ barvin.
dk. Tues–Thurs 3pm–10pm, Fri–Sat
3pm–11pm.

The menu at this rustic, relaxed
wine bar changes to match the wine
(rather than the other way around),
though the delicious charcuterie
and cheese platters always remain a
good bet. Expect to pay from 95kr
for a sandwich and up to 495kr for
a three-course meal.

Conditori La Glace

MAP P.32, POCKET MAP B12
Skoubogade 3 ☎ 33 14 46 46, ⓦ laglace.
dk. Mon–Fri 8.30am–6pm, Sat 9am–6pm,
Sun 10am–6pm (closed Sun April–Sept).

Traditional patisserie serving
beautifully crafted layer cakes and
pastries. Try the scrumptious HC
Hat cake, made with chocolate,
caramel mousse and lemon ganache
(62kr per slice).

Dalle Valle

MAP P.32, POCKET MAP B11
Fiolstræde 3–5 ☎ 33 93 29 29,

Conditori La Glace

W cafedallevalle.dk. Mon–Thurs
10am–11pm, Fri–Sat 10am–12pm, Sun
10am–10pm.
This spacious, bustling café is a
great place for sandwiches and
salads, with a few pasta dishes,
burgers and steaks also on offer;
scrummy hot wings, too (all
around 100–130kr). Also a popular
bar at night, with a DJ on Friday
and Saturday.

Det Lille Apotek

MAP P.32, POCKET MAP C11
Store Kannikestræde 15 ☎ 33 12 56 06,
W detlilleapotek.dk. Daily 11.30am–
midnight.
Dating back to 1720, the city's
oldest restaurant was once one
of Hans Christian Andersen's
favourite haunts, and with its
leadlight windows and hanging oil
lamps it still retains plenty of old-
time atmosphere. Highlights on the
menu of traditional Danish dishes
include *biksemad* (beef stew served
with pickled beetroot, cucumber
salad, fried eggs and slices of
rye bread; 98kr) for lunch and

flæskesteg (pork roast with crackling,
sugar-glazed potatoes, pickled red
cabbage and a thick, creamy sauce;
169kr) for dinner.

Europa 1989

MAP P.32, POCKET MAP D12
Amagertorv 1 ☎ 33 14 28 89,
W europa1989.dk. Mon–Thurs
7.45am–11pm, Fri & Sat 7.45am–midnight,
Sun 9am–10pm.
Large, fancy café on bustling
Højbro Plads serving excellent
coffee and cake, good breakfasts
(wholegrain porridge 39kr) and
brunch (daily until 3pm; 149kr).
It's also a popular after-work
spot, mostly for the drinks (the
beer selection is good) and their
excellent nibbles; try the shellfish
bisque or *bruschetta*.

Kong Hans Kælder

MAP P.32, POCKET MAP D12
Vingårdstræde 6 ☎ 33 11 68 68,
W konghans.dk. Wed–Sat 6pm–midnight.
Set in the cellar of a medieval
merchant's house, this Michelin-
starred place has a setting as

dramatic as it is romantic. The picture-perfect food is French-inspired with a twist. The five-course menu will set you back just 1700kr, excluding wine, while an à la carte main starts at 655kr.

Krogs Fiskerestaurant

MAP P.32, POCKET MAP C12

Gammel Strand 38 ☎ 33 15 89 15, ⓦ krogs. dk. Mon–Sat 11.30am–3pm & 5pm–10pm.

Though hidden behind the metro building chaos, the *grande dame* of the city's seafood restaurants – all high ceilings and meticulously dressed tables – is worth the hassle to get to. Half a dozen French oysters will set you back a couple of hundred kroner, or – if you're feeling flush – try the lobster with all the trimmings.

La Galette

MAP P.32, POCKET MAP B12

Larsbjørnsstræde 9 ☎ 33 32 37 90, ⓦ lagalette.dk. Mon–Sat noon–4pm & 5.30–11pm, Sun 1–10pm.

Informal place serving French-style buckwheat pancakes with both sweet and savoury fillings. Specialities include the Menez-Hom (95kr), filled with goat's cheese, walnuts and salad, and the Normande (60kr) with calvados-flambéed caramelized apples. In summer there's outdoor seating in the back yard.

L'education Nationale

MAP P.32, POCKET MAP B12

Larsbjørnsstræde 12 ☎ 33 91 53 60, ⓦ leducation.dk. Mon–Sun 11.30am–midnight.

Authentic and cosy, French-style bistro with tightly packed tables and French-speaking waiters. Lunchtime standards, such as omelette (105kr) and *moules marinières* (150kr), are reasonably priced. The evening menu is pricier but still good value (mains such as pheasant or sea bass around 235kr), and there's an excellent selection of wines.

Maven

MAP P.32, POCKET MAP D12

Nikolaj Plads 10 ☎ 32 20 11 00, ⓦ restaurantmaven.dk. Mon–Thurs 11.30am–midnight, Fri & Sat 11.30am–2am.

Inside the massive, red-brick Skt Nikolaj Kirke, a deconsecrated church that also hosts temporary exhibitions, *Maven* ("stomach") offers excellent French/Italian-inspired lunch and dinner menus as well as traditional lunchtime smørrebrød (198kr for a platter). Also a popular spot for evening drinks.

Norden

MAP P.32, POCKET MAP D12

Østergade 61 ☎ 33 11 77 91, ⓦ cafenorden. dk. Sun–Thurs 8.30am–11pm, Fri–Sat 8.30am–midnight.

A great pit stop on busy Strøget with fabulous home-made cakes and pancakes as well as beautifully assembled salads (from 180kr). There's also a fine selection of beer (including from the Jacobsen brewery; see page 81), a range of cocktails and a good few wines.

Paludan Bogcafé

MAP P.32, POCKET MAP B11

Fiolstræde 10–12 ☎ 33 15 06 75, ⓦ paludan-cafe.dk. Mon–Thurs 9am–10pm, Fri 9am–11pm, Sat 10am–11pm, Sun 10am–10pm.

With its free wi-fi and great-value meals – chicken tagliatelle (99kr) or the Paludan burger, for example – this bookshop-cum-café is a great student hangout. There's also good coffee and cheap beer.

Peder Oxe

MAP P.32, POCKET MAP C11

Gråbrødretorv 11 ☎ 33 11 00 77, ⓦ pederoxe.dk. Sun–Thurs 11am–10.30pm, Fri–Sat 11am–11pm.

One of several cafés and restaurants on this historic square (once home to a Greyfriars monastery), serving juicy, grilled organic burgers (from 165kr) and steaks (235kr) plus unlimited salads (95kr). The "dessert tapas" platter (140kr) is an exquisite experience in itself. Also a good place to go for drinks.

Pilekælderen

MAP P.32, POCKET MAP D11

Pilestræde 48 ☎ 33 33 00 26, ⓦ pilekaelderen.dk. Mon–Sun 11.30am–5pm.

Authentic, traditional lunchtime restaurant with thick stone walls and a low wood-beamed ceiling. It specializes in stunning smørrebrød, such as herring marinated in elderberry aquavit (79kr) – all home-made, of course.

Slotskælderen hos Gitte Kik

MAP P.32, POCKET MAP D12

Fortunstræde 4 ☎ 33 11 15 37, ⓦ slotskaelderen.dk. Tues–Sat 10am–7pm.

Cosy basement restaurant serving excellent traditional smørrebrød. Choose from the vast selection at the counter, such as delicious *rullepølse* (rolled pork with parsley and pepper), and the food will be brought to your table.

Sult

MAP P.32, POCKET MAP C10

Vognmagergade 8B ☎ 33 74 34 17, ⓦ restaurantsult.dk. Lunch: Tues–Fri 11.30am–4pm, Sat–Sun 9.30am–4pm, Dinner: Mon–Sat 5pm–10pm, Sun 5.30–9pm.

Occupying a high-ceilinged dining hall in the same building as the Danish Film Institute, *Sult* does simple well-prepared Danish dishes that don't cost the earth. Try the mouthwatering freshly cured ham from Jutland, served with grilled tomatoes and artichokes (129kr).

Vandkunsten sandwich & salatbar

MAP P.32, POCKET MAP C12

Rådhusstræde 17 ☎ 33 13 90 40, ⓦ vsandwich.dk. Mon–Fri 10am–4pm, Sat 11am–4pm.

Excellent place to grab a sandwich on the go (48–60kr), with lots of yummy vegetarian options (avocado mousse, mozzarella and so on) and freshly baked, crisp Italian rolls. Salads, which you can make up yourself, start at 44kr.

Yaffa

MAP P.32, POCKET MAP C11

Europa 1989

Det Lille Apotek

Gråbrødtorv 16 📞 71 72 66 11, 🌐 yaffa.dk.
Mon–Sat 11.30am–midnight.
A hit with both food and design
bloggers, warming Eastern
Mediterranean and Middle Eastern
dishes are served in a setting
of mismatched wooden chairs,
concrete surfaces and bistro-style
tiled floors. A specialist in sharing-
food, the 12-course dinner menu
will fill your table with octopus,
duck hearts, samosas and chili
hummus (350kr per person). A
more simple five-dish lunch menu
costs 135kr. Serving staff have a
passion for wine too, so linger after
your meal to savour an extra pour.

Bars

1105

MAP P.32, POCKET MAP D11
Kristen Bernikows Gade 4 📞 33 93 11
05, 🌐 1105.dk. Wed, Thurs 7pm–2am, Fri
4pm–2am, Sat 6pm–2am.
Cool, elegant, low-lit cocktail bar,
where the mixologists wear crisp
white lab coats. *1105* has made a
name for itself with the creation
of the Copenhagen cocktail, a
delicious mix of genever (Dutch
gin), cherry liqueur, lime juice and
a host of secret ingredients.

Bo-Bi Bar

MAP P.32, POCKET MAP C11
Klareboderne 4 📞 33 12 55 43. Mon–Sat
noon–2am, Sun 2pm–2am.
This Baroque, red hole-in-the-wall
is one of the city's most authentic
watering holes. Opened in 1917,
it sports Copenhagen's oldest bar
counter and attracts a refreshingly
boho clientele of writers, students
and intellectuals – great for people-
watching. Serves cheap bottles of
great Danish and Czech beers as
well as local schnapps.

Charlie's Bar

MAP P.32, POCKET MAP D11
Pilestræde 33 📞 33 22 22 89. Mon & Tues
2pm–midnight, Wed noon–1am, Thurs–Sat
noon–2am, Sun 2–10pm.
Packed, small and smoky,
Copenhagen's only UK-style
pub – even boasting Casque Mark
accreditation – draws in the crowds
night after night for its ever-changing
range of British ales and ciders.

K-Bar

MAP P.32, POCKET MAP D12
Ved Stranden 20 📞 33 91 92 22, 🌐 k-bar.
dk. Mon–Thurs 4pm–1am, Fri & Sat
4pm–2am.
Tucked round the corner from
Højbro Plads square, this funky

cocktail bar has deep, cosy sofas into which punters can happily sink as they sip the beautiful concoctions of owner Kirsten – hence the K. Try the unusual and moreish Rissitini, made with gin, sake, lychee liqueur and ginger.

The Living Room

MAP P.32, POCKET MAP B12
Larsbjørnsstræde 17 ⓘ 33 32 66 10. ⓦ thelivingroom.dk. Mon–Thurs 9am–11pm, Fri 9am–2am, Sat 10am–2am, Sun 10am–7pm.

Laidback corner bar on chilled Larsbjørnsstræde, with tables outside and soft sofas in the basement. It's a great place to go for freshly squeezed juices, organic wines, coffee and affordable cocktails.

Ruby

MAP P.32, POCKET MAP C12
Nybrogade 10 ⓘ 33 93 12 03, ⓦ rby.dk. Mon–Sat 4pm–2am, Sun 6pm–2am.

Set in what appears to be for all the world an unassuming ground-floor apartment, with comfy leather armchairs and no obvious signage, this is possibly the city's best cocktail bar. Try the signature Rapscallion – a Scottish take on the Manhattan, with Talisker over a sweet PX sherry.

Music venues

Drop Inn

MAP P.32, POCKET MAP B12
Kompagnistræde 34 ⓘ 33 11 24 04, ⓦ drop-inn.dk. Mon–Tues noon–1am, Wed–Thurs noon–2am. Priced per event.

Small folk, blues and rock venue, with tables spilling onto the pavement during hot summer months and a good selection of international beers. Music from 10/10.30pm most nights (usually free during the week; from 30kr Sat & Sun).

Jazzhus Montmartre

MAP P.32, POCKET MAP D11
Store Regnegade 19A ⓘ 70 26 32 67, ⓦ jazzhusmontmartre.dk. Doors open at 5.30pm.

Intimate, not-for-profit jazz club, which reopened in 2010 after having placed Copenhagen firmly on the international jazz map in the 1950s when it hosted legends such as Dexter Gordon and Stan Getz. Concerts two to three nights a week (100–350kr).

La Fontaine

MAP P.32, POCKET MAP C12
Kompagnistræde 11 ⓘ 33 11 60 98, ⓦ lafontaine.dk. Daily 7pm–5am.

As Copenhagen's oldest jazz venue, *La Fontaine* has for decades been where jazz musicians make for on their nights off. It's small and packed, with live gigs at the weekend (Fri–Sat from 10pm, Sun from 9pm; entry from 100kr).

Musikcaféen

MAP P.32, POCKET MAP C12
Rådhusstræde 13 ⓘ 21 51 21 51, ⓦ huset-kbh.dk.

On the third floor of the Huset cultural centre, this is the place to hear up-and-coming bands before they become famous. Gigs most nights, starting at 8 or 9pm (40–150kr).

Bo-Bi Bar

Slotsholmen

Encircled by Indre By on three sides and abutting the Inner Harbour on the fourth, the flat, diminutive island of Slotsholmen has been the country's seat of power for almost a thousand years. It was here, in 1167, that Bishop Absalon founded a castle to protect the village's herring traders from Wendish pirates. The area is anchored by the commanding and glum-looking Christiansborg Slot; home to the Danish parliament and the royals' reception rooms, it's the fifth incarnation of a royal dwelling on this site. Other highlights within the palace complex include the extravagant Royal Stables and riding ground, the elegant Palace Chapel and, next door, the colourful Thorvaldsens Museum, while on the opposite side of Christiansborg the Daniel Libeskind-designed interior of the Danish Jewish Museum and, on the waterfront, the gleaming Black Diamond extension to the Royal Library provide more modern architectural draws.

Folketing (Danish Parliament)

MAP P.46, POCKET MAP D13
Christiansborg ☏ 33 37 32 21,
ⓦ thedanishparliament.dk. Tours (free)
most Sundays at 1pm (tickets available
from 10am and online). Sittings roughly
Oct to mid-June: Tues & Wed from 1pm,
Thurs & Fri from 10am.

Royal Reception Rooms

Occupying the southern half of the three-winged palace of Christiansborg, the **Folketing** (Danish parliament) is a must for fans of the cult TV political drama series *Borgen*, set in and around the palace. You can watch the debates in the principal parliamentary chamber, the **Folketingssal**, when in session – ring the visitors' entrance bell, and, if spaces are available, you'll be taken through security checks to the public galleries – though bear in mind that debates are not nearly as animated as the UK equivalent. Alternatively the Sunday English-language **tours** cover the history of Danish democracy as well as the palace's colourful history, taking you down the long Vandrehal where the much revered original Danish constitution from 1849 is displayed in a silver chest.

Royal Reception Rooms

MAP P.46, POCKET MAP D12
Christiansborg ☏ 33 92 64 92,

Royalty Danish style

The Danish Royal Family stands as one of the oldest monarchies in the world. The current monarch, Her Majesty Queen Margrethe II, traces her lineage all the way back to Harald Bluetooth, the famous Viking chieftain and first king of a united Denmark over a thousand years ago. The Royal Family remains an extremely popular institution in Denmark. Crown Prince Frederik has been regularly voted "Dane of The Year", while his Tasmanian-born wife Princess Mary is both vaunted style icon and global advocate of women's health. Prince Henrick, husband of Queen Margrethe, died on February 13th, 2018 aged 83 after several months of poor health.

ⓦ **christiansborg.dk. April–Oct daily 9am–5pm, Nov–March Tues–Sun 10am–5pm,closed during royal functions and on Mondays from Nov–March. 95kr, 160kr for combined ticket with Ruins under Christiansborg and Royal Stables. Tours at 3pm.**

Although it was built as a royal palace, the royals have never actually lived at Christiansborg, favouring the slightly more open and accessible Amalienborg. A section of the northern wing of the palace is, however, still in royal use for official functions as the **Royal Reception Rooms** (Det Kongelige Repræsentationslokaler) accessed via the Inner Courtyard. Sure to impress any visiting dignitaries, all the rooms are beautifully adorned. An intricate marble frieze depicting Alexander's march into Babylon by Thorvaldsen (see page 47) was recovered from the previous Christiansborg and following skilful restoration is on display in the Alexander Hall. The marble walls in the oval Throne Room are clad in delicate silks from Lyon, while on the ceiling a magnificent painting depicts the origins of the national flag. Best of all, however, is the long Great Hall, lined with seventeen magnificent tapestries by Bjørn Nørgaard (also famous for the mosaics on Strøget; see page 30). A fiftieth birthday present for the current Queen, they depict the country's history from the Viking Age to the present. See if you can spot The Beatles and Mao Zedong.

Ruinerne Under Christiansborg (castle ruins)

MAP P.46, POCKET MAP D12
Christiansborg ⓘ 33 92 64 92,
ⓦ **christiansborg.dk. Daily 10am–5pm (closed Mon Oct–April). Tours Sat at noon. 50kr, 120kr for combined ticket with Royal Reception Rooms and Royal Stables.**
The **ruins** of Slotsholmen's two earliest castles have been excavated and now form part of an underground **exhibition** beneath Christiansborg, accessed via a stairwell from the main entrance portal. A walkway tracks the foundations of Bishop Absalon's original castle, while the extant highlight of its successor, Københavns Slot, which was put up in the late fourteenth century, is the foundations of its notorious Blue Tower prison where King Christian IV's daughter Leonora Christine was kept captive for 22 years, supposedly due to her blinding beauty.

Ridebane (Royal Stables)

MAP P.46, POCKET MAP C13
Christiansborg Ridebane 12 ⓘ 33 92 64 92, ⓦ **christiansborg.dk. April–June & Aug–Oct daily 1.30–4pm, July 10am–5pm, Nov–March Tues–Sun 1.30–4pm. Tours in English Sat at 2pm. 50kr, 120kr for combined ticket with Royal Reception Rooms and Ruins under Christiansborg.**

Beyond the Inner Courtyard, the **Ridebane** (Royal Stables) and surrounding riding ground are all that's left of the opulent Baroque palace that stood here from 1738 until it burnt to the ground 56 years later. If you arrive around mid-morning you stand a good chance of seeing the Queen's horses being exercised either in the outdoor riding arena, or, if you poke your head in discreetly, in the lavish Riding Hall.

The **Museet Kongelige Stalde og Kareter** (Museum of Royal Stables and Coaches), in the southern flank, houses the extravagant marble-clad stables where a few lucky horses are still kept, alongside the royal collection of gilded carriages plus the previous king's beautiful old Bentley.

To the west as you exit the museum, the Baroque **Marmorbroen** (Marble Bridge) linking Slotsholmen with mainland Indre By was the original palace's main approach.

Christiansborg Slotskirke (Palace Chapel)

MAP P.46, POCKET MAP D12
Prins Jørgens Gård 1 Ⓦ christiansborg.
dk. July daily 10am–5pm; Aug–June Sun
10am–5pm. Tours in Danish Sun at 2pm.
Fully restored following a catastrophic fire in 1992 the Neoclassical **Palace Chapel** is all that remains of the second Christiansborg palace, which like its predecessor also burnt to the ground some fifty-odd years after completion (in 1833). The palace was said to be the most lavish of all the Christiansborg incarnations, though the church's elegant and light interior – topped by a vast white dome with four angels in relief seemingly floating beneath – is exquisite Classical simplicity itself. Still put to use for the opening of parliament

CAFÉ AND RESTAURANT	
Café Øieblikket	2
Søren K	1

Slotsholmen

Royal Stables

service and for the occasional royal event, the church is also used for organ practice by the Danish Music Conservatory.

Thorvaldsens Museum

MAP P.46, POCKET MAP C12
Bertel Thorvaldsens Plads 2 ☎ 33 32 15 32, ⓦ thorvaldsensmuseum.dk. Tues–Sun 10am–5pm. 70kr, Free admission on Wednesdays.

Dedicated to Denmark's most internationally celebrated sculptor, the **Thorvaldsens Museum** is an absorbing place to while away a few hours. You certainly won't miss the grand Neoclassical edifice, overlooking the picturesque Frederiksholms Kanal, within which it's housed: with its striking ochre facade, and unusual slanting doors and window frames, it stands out as one of the city's most original buildings.

Having trained in Copenhagen, **Bertel Thorvaldsen** (1770–1844) spent forty years fulfilling high-profile commissions in Rome before returning triumphantly in 1839 – an event depicted on the huge frieze painted on the canal-facing side of the building. Thorvaldsen spent the last few years of his life fulfilling commissions in Copenhagen, and his work can be seen in both Vor Frue Kirke and Christiansborg Slotskirke.

Inside, richly decorated walls and mosaic floors provide a fitting backdrop for the vast collection of Thorvaldsen's works on the ground floor, from huge marble sculptures to sketches and grubby plaster casts with the sculptor's own original marks. Highlights include the intimate *Cupid and Psyche* and Thorvaldsen's own self-portrait in stone. Upstairs, the sculptor's fine collection of Greek, Roman and Egyptian antiquities is on display.

Krigsmuseet

MAP P.46, POCKET MAP F8
Tøjhusgade 3 ☎ 33 92 70 85, ⓦ natmus.dk, Tues–Sun 10am–5pm. 80kr, under 18s free.

Part of the National Museum (see page 28), the **Danish War Museum** showcases both famous battles from the past and more recent battles, most remarkable, though, is the 156m arched hall housing the cannon collection, said to be the longest such hall in Europe. The exhibitions range form a walk-through relaying the Danish experience in war-torn Afghanistan,

Thorvaldsens Museum

to Cold War posters. Most
remarkable, though, is the 156m
arched hall housing the cannon
collection, said to be the longest
such hall in Europe. The former
Orlogsmuseet (Royal Danish Naval
museum) closed down in 2015;
as a result the Krigsmuseet houses
incredibly detailed, to-scale ship
models from sixteenth-century
galleons, modern submarines play
and other historical warships from
the Danish navy.

Børsen

MAP P.46, POCKET MAP D13
Børsgade Ⓦ borsbygningen.dk.
A fanciful riot of gables, pinnacles
and grey-green copper, the red-
brick **Børsen** building is one of
the more remarkable monuments
of Christian IV's reign. It's for
its wonderfully whimsical spire –
made up of the intertwined tails
of four sculpted dragons – that
the building is best known. The
dragons supposedly protect the
Børsen from attack and fire, and
seem to be fulfilling their duties
quite successfully as the building
has survived many a skirmish as
those around it have burnt to the
ground. Although ownership of
the building has long since passed

to the Chamber of Commerce (it's
not open to the public), the dragon
spire remains the official symbol of
the Danish stock exchange.

Dansk Jødisk Museum

MAP P.46, POCKET MAP D13
Proviantpassagen 6 Ⓣ 33 11 22 18,
Ⓦ jewmus.dk. June–Aug Tues–Sun
10am–5pm; Sept–May Tues–Fri 1–4pm,
Sat & Sun noon–5pm. 60kr for one exhibit;
75kr for multiple exhibits.
Opened in 2004 and designed
by Daniel Libeskind, architect
of the new World Trade Center
site in New York, the **Danish
Jewish Museum** retells the story
of Jewry in Denmark from their
arrival in the seventeenth century
at the invitation of Christian
IV up to the gruesome wartime
period. Housed in the Galajhus
(Royal Boat House), the building
gives no indication from the
outside of its subtly disorientating
interior, a labyrinth of fractured
passageways and sloping floors
reminiscent of Libeskind's more
famous Jewish Museum in Berlin.
The museum's layout corresponds
to the interlocking characters of
the Hebrew word *Mitzvah* ("good
deed"), a reference to the Danes'
smuggling of seven thousand Jews

hidden away in fishing boats across to sanctuary in Sweden during World War II (see page 54).

The exhibition itself is divided into five sections, focusing on different aspects of Danish-Jewish life. The most captivating of these is the Mitzvah section itself, which recounts the plight of Danish Jews during Nazi occupation. There are some heartfelt and touching letters and photos from refugees in Sweden on show, and hand-drawn sketches of horrible episodes at the Theresienstadt concentration camp (in what's now the Czech Republic), where 481 Danish Jews were sent.

Den Sorte Diamant (The Black Diamond)

MAP P.46, POCKET MAP D13
Søren Kierkegaards Plads 1 ☏ 33 47 47 47, ⓦ kb.dk. Mon–Sat 8am–9pm. Access to all museums 40kr. Tours Sat 3pm 60kr (including access to all museums).
Den Sorte Diamant (The Black Diamond), a monumental slab of black Zimbabwean granite and glass that leans over (and glitters magically in) the waters of the Inner Harbour below, is one of the city's great modern architectural icons. Completed in

1999, the building is an extension to the Italian-inspired **Kongelige Bibliotek** (Royal Library) (1906), to which it is connected by a futuristic glass-enclosed bridge.

The building houses an auditorium with outstanding acoustics, museums dedicated to photography and cartoon art, and a changing display of works from the Royal Library's collection. You're free to wander about the building at will, though some of the exhibitions (see below) do charge an entrance fee. Among its attractions are the National Museum of Photography, which – in addition to some 50,000 photos in its collection, dating back to the birth of photography in 1839 – hosts interesting changing exhibitions of both modern and historical photographers (Mon–Sat 10am–7pm; 40kr).

The old library building behind is less accessible to the general public and best experienced on the **guided tours**, which take in both buildings. Highlights of the Royal Library include several of the atmospheric old study halls, one which features the city's earliest grid-powered electric lamps.

Café and restaurant

Café Øieblikket

MAP P.46, POCKET MAP D13
Søren Kierkegaards Plads 1 ☏ 33 47 41 06, ⓦ oieblikket.dk. Mon–Fri 8am–7pm, Sat 9am–6pm.
A popular venue among the city's studious, this café, located in the light and airy foyer of the Black Diamond, serves excellent coffee and a tempting array of mouthwatering cakes. There are deckchairs on the Inner Harbour quayside in summer, too.

Søren K

MAP P.46, POCKET MAP D13
Kierkegaards Plads 1 ☏ 33 47 49 49, ⓦ soerenk.dk. Mon–Sat 11am–4pm & 5.30–11pm.
Immaculate and minimalist, the Black Diamond's upmarket waterfront restaurant boasts beautifully dressed tables lined up along the quayside walkway. It's packed throughout the day, with champagne and oysters (120kr) the lunchtime favourite, while in the evenings there's a five-course menu (435kr) focused around local produce. *Borgen* fans will notice that this is where many of PM Birgitte Nyborg's external meetings take place.

Nyhavn and Frederiksstaden

Packed with busy bars and restaurants, canalside Nyhavn attracts thousands of visitors thanks to its pretty postcard setting. To its north are the elegant Rococo houses and immaculately straight streets of Frederiksstaden, built as a grand symbol of Frederik V's reign. The huge dome of the Marmorkirken dominates the skyline, while three main north–south streets divide the area: Store Kongensgade, lined with galleries, restaurants and high-end shops; quieter Bredgade; and partially cobbled Amaliegade, which bisects the palaces of Amalienborg – the royals' official winter residence. All three streets lead up to Christian IV's impressive defensive fortress, the grass-bastioned Kastellet, close to which is a pair of inspirational museums. Finally, perched on a lonely rock off the Kastellet's northern edge, is the city's most famous icon – the diminutive Little Mermaid.

Nyhavn

MAP P.52, POCKET MAP E11–F11

Picturesque **Nyhavn** is perhaps the city's most popular tourist hangout. The "new harbour" was created in 1671 to link Kongens Nytorv to the sea – the earliest

Nyhavn

of the townhouses, no. 9, dates from this period – and has been home to some famous residents – Hans Christian Andersen lived for a while at no. 67. The area has not always been so salubrious, however: Nyhavn went through a long period as the city's most disreputable red-light district before its transformation into the welcoming visitor haunt of today. On a sunny summer's evening (there are outdoor heaters in winter) it's easy to see the attraction of sipping a beer while gazing over the historic yachts (usually) moored in the harbour. Be warned, though: food and drink do not come cheap.

Kunsthal Charlottenborg

MAP P.52, POCKET MAP E11

Nyhavn 2 ☏ 33 74 46 39, ⓦ charlottenborg. dk. Tues–Fri noon–8pm, Sat–Sun 11am–5pm; 90kr, Free admission on Wednesdays after 5pm.

Located between Kongens Nytorv and Nyhavn (and with entrances on both) the **Kunsthal Charlottenborg** is housed in one

Amalienborg

of the least prepossessing palaces in Copenhagen. Built for the illegitimate son of Frederik III, it has since 1754 been home to the Royal Danish Academy of Fine Arts. There are no permanent displays but changing exhibitions of modern art are put on in the newer building (added in 1883) behind. One such exhibition in 1971, about the new hippie movement, triggered the founding of Christiania (see page 73).

Amalienborg
MAP P.52, POCKET MAP F10

The winter residence of the Danish royal family, **Amalienborg** is made up four almost identical Rococo palaces, arranged symmetrically around an octagonal courtyard that centres on a statue of Frederik V on horseback. Designed by royal architect Nicolai Eigtved in 1750, the palaces were originally built for (and funded by) wealthy Danish nobles, though the royals commandeered them following the devastating fire at Christiansborg in 1794. Today all four palaces are named both after their original benefactor and a subsequent resident royal. The Queen lives in Christian IX's Palæ – or Schacks Palæ – with her husband Prince Henrik, while Frederik VIII's Palæ (Brockdorffs Palæ) is home to Crown Prince Frederik and family; both are completely off-limits.

Note too that **Christian VII's Palæ** (also known as Moltkes Palæ), whose fabulous Great Hall is considered to be one of the finest Rococo rooms in Europe, is unfortunately no longer open to the public.

You can, however, visit Christian VIII's Palæ (Levetzaus Palæ), the first floor of which contains the **Amalienborgmuseet** (Amalienborg Museum; May–Oct daily 10am–4pm; Nov–April Tues–Sun 11am–4pm; 90kr; Ⓦamalienborgmuseet.dk), devoted to more recent royal history. The studies of each of

Nyhavn and Frederiksstaden

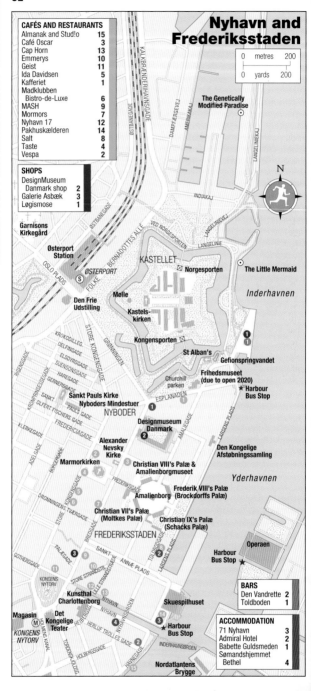

CAFÉS AND RESTAURANTS

Almanak and Stud!o	15
Café Oscar	3
Cap Horn	13
Emmerys	10
Geist	11
Ida Davidsen	5
Kafferiet	1
Madklubben	
Bistro-de-Luxe	6
MASH	9
Mormors	7
Nyhavn 17	12
Pakhuskælderen	14
Salt	8
Taste	4
Vespa	2

SHOPS

DesignMuseum	
Danmark shop	2
Galerie Asbæk	3
Løgismose	1

0 metres 200
0 yards 200

N

The Genetically Modified Paradise

KALKBRÆNDERIHAVNSGADE
DAMPFÆRGEVEJ
AMERIKAKAJ
LANGELINIEKAJ
ØSTBANEGADE
INDIAKAJ
VED NORGESPORTEN
LANGELINIE
LANGELINIEVEJ

Garnisons Kirkegård

Østerport Station

ØSTERPORT
OSLO PLADS
FOLKE
BERNADOTTES ALLÉ

KASTELLET

Nørgesporten

The Little Mermaid

Inderhavnen

Den Frie Udstilling

Mølle

Kastels- kirken

Kongensporten

St Alban's

Gefionspringvandet

Frihedsmuseet (due to open 2020)

★ Harbour Bus Stop

KROKODILLEG.
DELFINGADE
ELSDYRSGADE
SUENSONSGADE
HAREGADE
GERNERSGADE
STORE KONGENSGADE
GRØNNINGEN
RIGENSGADE
KRONPRINSESSEGADE
SANKT OLFERT FISCHERS GADE
PAULS GADE
KLERKEGADE
FREDERICIAGADE
ADEL GADE
BORGERGADE
STORE KONGENSGADE
DRONNINGENS TVÆRGADE

Sankt Pauls Kirke
Nyboders Mindestuer

NYBODER

Churchill parken

ESPLANADEN

Designmuseum Danmark

Alexander Nevsky Kirke

Marmorkirken

Christian VIII's Palæ & Amalienborgmuseet

AMALIEGADE

LARSENS PLADS

Den Kongelige Afstøbningssamling

Frederik VIII's Palæ (Brockdorffs Palæ)

Amalienborg

Christian VII's Palæ (Moltkes Palæ)

Christian IX's Palæ (Schacks Palæ)

FREDERIKSSTADEN

FREDERIKSGADE
BREDGADE

Yderhavnen

Operaen

Harbour Bus Stop ★

BARS

Den Vandrette	2
Toldboden	1

GOTHERSGADE
PALÆGADE
STORE STRANDSTR.
SANKT ANNÆ PLADS
TOLDBODGADE
LARSENS PLADS

Kunsthal Charlottenborg

KONGENS NYTORV

Magasin

Det Kongelige Teater

KONGENS NYTORV

LILLE STRANDSTR.
HEIBERGSG.
NYHAVN
HERLUF TROLLES GADE
HAVNEGADE
TORDENSKJOLDSG.
HOLBERGSGADE

Skuespilhuset

Harbour Bus Stop

INDERHAVNSBROEN

Nordatlantens Brygge

ACCOMMODATION

71 Nyhavn	3
Admiral Hotel	2
Babette Guldsmeden	1
Sømandshjemmet	
Bethel	4

the last three kings have been fully reconstructed (complete with vast pipe collections and family portraits), giving a flavour of their modern if by no means luxurious lifestyles.

Outside on the courtyard, the **changing of the guard** ceremony at noon each day is a great hit with kids. Childish souls may try to see if they can induce the bearskin-wearing guard to flinch – chances are they won't.

Skuespilhuset

MAP P.52, POCKET MAP F11
Sankt Annæ Plads 36 ☎ 33 69 69 33,
Ⓦ kglteater.dk. Guided tours (75min)
100kr; check website for times.

The **Skuespilhuset** (Playhouse), around the corner from Nyhavn, is unanimously agreed to be one of the city's most elegant new buildings. It has a stunning position on the Inner Harbour, with a projecting upper storey that appears to be balancing precariously over the water's edge. A copper-clad tower thrusts skyward from within, while a wooden promenade encircles

the building and doubles as an outdoor café. To see the inside, either join one of the irregular tours or take in a performance – although productions here are almost exclusively staged in Danish.

Marmorkirken

MAP P.52, POCKET MAP E10
Frederiksgade 4 ☎ 33 15 01 44. Mon–Thurs
& Sat 10am–5pm, Fri & Sun noon–5pm.
Free.

Modelled on St Peter's in the Vatican, the **Marmorkirken** (Marble Church), which is properly called Frederiks Kirke, took almost 150 years to complete. Originally commissioned by Frederik V in 1749, the church's construction was halted twenty years later due to lack of funds, and only with financial support from a leading Danish industrial magnate, C.F. Tietgen, was it completed – using cheaper marble – in 1894, having languished in ruins for more than a century. You can join a tour to climb the 260 steps to the top of the **dome (35kr)**, from which there are spectacular views down over

The Royal Danish Playhouse

The Danish Resistance

Despite pledging to remain neutral during World War II Denmark was occupied by German forces from April 9, 1940 until May 1945. While the occupation was not the bloodbath that unfurled elsewhere in Europe, **resistance groups** nonetheless sprung up, among them the "Churchill Club", a group of schoolboys who sabotaged German vehicles, and the Hvidsten Group (subject of a hit 2012 Danish film) who distributed British weapons from secret airdrops. One of the proudest moments of this period was the clandestine evacuation in October 1943 of the vast majority of Denmark's seven thousand Jews to safety in neutral Sweden; almost everyone seems to have an uncle or grandfather who was somehow involved.

Until recently the best place to get to grips with the Danish wartime experience was the **Frihedsmuseet** (Museum of Freedom, or Museum of Danish Resistance) at 7 Churchillparken. Sadly, on May 5, 2013, the museum was ravaged by fire – an incident attributed to arson. Fortunately, no archival records or artefacts – such as Himmler's eye patch, taken off him by the Allies as he was captured trying to flee in disguise – were lost in the blaze. At the time of press, construction of a new building was still in the design phase. In the meantime the Ryvangen Memorial Park in Hellerup commemorates resistance fighters executed by the Nazis.

diminutive Copenhagen beneath you and towards the Swedish coastline in the distance. Note too how the relatively new Operaen across the harbour has been aligned perfectly with the Marmorkirken and Amalienborg.

Designmuseum Danmark

MAP P.52, POCKET MAP G6
Bredgade 68 ⓘ 33 18 56 56,
Ⓦ designmuseum.dk. Tues–Sun 10am–6pm, Wed 10am–9pm. 100kr.
Formerly the Kunstindustrimuseet, and not to be confused with the (now closed) Danish Design Center, this temple to (predominantly Danish) design occupies the four wings of the old Frederiks Hospital. Pride of place among the permanent exhibitions goes to the section on twentieth-century **Danish applied art and craft**, which takes in the full range of the iconic designs that have given Denmark its international

reputation – from Arne Jacobsen's Ant chair to Kaj Bojesen's classic wooden toy monkey and Ole Kirk Christiansen's Lego brick. Elsewhere, the collection traces the history of European and Asian applied and decorative art, with the emphasis on how it relates to the development of Danish design. The Asian collection is particularly strong – ranging from Japanese sword paraphernalia to Chinese Ming vases. Check out the selection in the museum shop (see page 56) if you fancy taking any pieces home with you.

Kastellet

MAP P.52, POCKET MAP G5
Daily 6am–10pm.
Surrounded by grassy ramparts and a series of moats, Copenhagen's quaint **Kastellet** (Citadel) is one of the best-preserved star-shaped fortresses in northern Europe. Brainchild of Christian IV and

completed by Frederik III, it was constructed to defend the city from all sides, including from the city itself in case of rebellion. Its terraced rows of immaculate, mansard-roofed barracks, painted in warm red hues, are still occupied by troops, making this also one of Europe's oldest functioning military bases. The granite war memorial in its southwest corner, dedicated to the many Danish soldiers who have been lost in action around the world since 1948, was unveiled in 2011.

The Little Mermaid

MAP P.52, POCKET MAP G5

Sitting on a boulder in the Inner Harbour off the northern edge of Kastellet, looking forlornly out to sea, **The Little Mermaid** (*Den lille havfrue*) is the city's most famous symbol. The embodiment of Hans Christian Andersen's fairy-tale character, she was created by Danish sculptor Edvard Eriksen in 1913 and paid for by Carlsberg brewery magnate Carl Jakobsen. Considering her diminutive size and somewhat vacant facial expression, the cynical observer might find it difficult to fathom her appeal to the busloads of tourists that visit her 24 hours a day, though her tragic tale of doomed love for her dream prince still has a powerful hold on the Danish imagination. The statue has not had an easy life, either. She's been the frequent victim of radical groups, covered in paint several times and beheaded twice.

A more recent addition a few hundred metres to the north along the waterfront at Langeliniekaj, the Little Mermaid's iconoclastic "ugly sister" is far more entertaining. Part of Bjørn Nørgaard's sculpture garden **The Genetically Modified Paradise**, she sits like her older sister on a boulder in the water, but with body and limbs grotesquely elongated and contorted – perhaps a truer rendition of Andersen's Little Mermaid's suffering than the original statue.

Designmuseum Danmark

NYHAVN AND FREDERIKSSTADEN

Shops

DesignMuseum Danmark shop

MAP P.52, POCKET MAP G6
Bredgade 68 ☎ 33 18 56 76,
Ⓦ designmuseum.dk. Tues–Sun
10am–6pm, Wed 10am–9pm.

The Design Museum's shop is a
great place for industrial design,
and to pick up ceramics, glass,
textiles and jewellery, all Danish-
made. Check out Kaj Bojesen's
wooden animal toys and the
beautiful glassware by Holmegaard.

Galerie Asbæk

MAP P.52, POCKET MAP E11
Bredgade 23 ☎ 33 15 40 04, Ⓦ asbaek.dk.
Tues–Fri 11am–6pm, Sat 11am–4pm.

This well-known art gallery sells
works by some of the country's
leading contemporary artists,
including CoBrA painter Carl
Henning-Pedersen (aka the
"Scandinavian Chagall") and
photographer Niels Bonde.

Cap Horn

Løgismose

MAP P.52, POCKET MAP G5
Nordre Toldbod 16 ☎ 33 32 93 32,
Ⓦ loegismose.dk. Mon–Fri 10am–7pm, Sat
10am–5pm.

A cornucopia of fabulous wines and
spirits is on sale at this deli on the
Innerhavnen, as well as delicious
cheeses and charcuterie from
France, Spain and Italy. It's also an
outlet for heavenly Summerbird
chocolate (see page 83).

Cafés and restaurants

Café Oscar

MAP P.52, POCKET MAP G6
Bredgade 58 ☎ 33 12 50 10, Ⓦ cafeoscar.
dk. Daily 10am–10pm.

Upmarket corner café a short
walk from Amalienborg, serving a
selection of excellent smørrebrød
(from 98kr), burgers, sandwiches
and salads, plus a meat-focused
evening menu. Fabulous food

aside, it's to be seen hobnobbing with the rich and famous that most people come.

Cap Horn

MAP P.52, POCKET MAP E11
Nyhavn 21 ☎ 33 12 85 04, ⓦ caphorn.
dk. Sun–Thurs 9am–11pm, Fri–Sat 9am–
midnight.

The best choice among the long row of overpriced restaurants along Nyhavns Kanal, *Cap Horn* serves largely organic fare, including juicy burgers (140kr) and always one or two seafood options (from 189kr).

Emmerys

MAP P.52, POCKET MAP E11
Store Strandstræde 21 ☎ 51 85 77 19,
ⓦ emmerys.dk. Mon–Fri 7.30am–6pm, Sat
& Sun 8am–4pm.

Part of an ever-expanding chain of café-bakeries, *Emmerys* is famous for its slow-risen organic bread, which you sample in sandwiches or as part of a breakfast platter. It's a great coffee stop, too, and treat yourself to a superb gooey brownie while you're at it.

Geist

MAP P.52, POCKET MAP E11
Kongens Nytorv 8 ☎ 33 13 37 13,
ⓦ restaurantgeist.dk. Daily 11.30am–3pm
& 5.30pm–1am.

This hip but unpretentious (and well-priced) spot is presided over by ex-*Paustian* chef Bo Bech. In the centre, the open kitchen has stools around it for diners' observation, while the thirty-dish menu focuses on some inventive fusions such as grilled octopus and strawberries (199kr) or vanilla ice cream, served with olives, cinnamon and liquorice (99kr).

Ida Davidsen

MAP P.52, POCKET MAP E10
Store Kongensgade 70 ☎ 33 91 36 55,
ⓦ idadavidsen.dk. Mon–Fri 10.30am–5pm;
closed July.

When the craving strikes for smørrebrød, it's to *Ida Davidsen*

that the Danish royals decamp – and the elaborately assembled smørrebrød (from 85kr) and sandwiches are indeed fit for a king. *Dyrlægens natmad* (literally "vet's midnight snack" – buttered rye bread smeared with liver pâté and topped with aspic and a slice of salted beef) is a particular highlight.

Kafferiet

MAP P.52, POCKET MAP G6
Esplanaden 44 ☎ 33 93 93 04, ⓦ kafferiet.
net. Mon–Fri 7.30am–6pm, Sat & Sun
9.30am–6pm.

Colourful and cosy little coffee shop across from Kastellet with a few tables inside and a couple outside on the street, too. There's delightful coffee and home-made cakes, plus interesting Italian confectionery: sweets from Pastiglie Leone and Amarelli liquorice.

Madklubben Bistro-de-Luxe

MAP P.52, POCKET MAP E10
Store Kongensgade 66 ☎ 33 32 32 34,
ⓦ madklubben.dk. Mon–Sat 5.30pm–
midnight.

Branch of the wildly popular Danish/French bistro chain that offers simple, tasty food in a relaxed atmosphere. You choose one, two or three courses and the price is 125kr, 175 or 225. Try the roasted duck leg with figs or 300g ribeye.

MASH

MAP P.52, POCKET MAP E11
Bredgade 20 ☎ 33 13 93 00, ⓦ mashsteak.
dk. Lunch Mon–Fri noon–3pm. Dinner
Mon–Wed & Sun 5.30–10pm; Thurs–Sat
5.30–11pm.

MASH stands for Modern American Steak House, which is exactly what you get – juicy steaks in a US diner setting. Starters (115kr) range from snails with garlic to half a grilled lobster and the steaks (from 360kr) come in all shapes and sizes – from Uruguayan tenderloin to American bone-in ribeye, via Aussie Wagyu fillet.

Mormors

MAP P.52, POCKET MAP E10
Bredgade 45 ⓣ 33 16 07 00, ⓦ mormors.dk. Mon–Fri 8.30am–5pm, Sat–Sun 10am–5pm.

A homely pit stop, *Mormors* ("Grandma's") easily lives up to its name with its warm and welcoming feel. There's hot soup for the cold winter months (55kr), a range of freshly made juices (42kr), sandwiches galore and a counter full of delicious cakes. Park yourself in one of the window seats inside, or at the pavement tables out front.

Nyhavn 17

MAP P.52, POCKET MAP E11
Nyhavn 17 ⓣ 33 12 54 19, ⓦ nyhavn17.dk. Sun–Thurs 10am–1.30am, Fri & Sat 10am–2am.

Housed in a 17th-century building with a big red neon sign on the front, it isn't hard to miss. Inside it's French bistro-meets old-fashioned bar, decorated with vintage photographs and nautical ornaments. The fish and chips (189kr) are a favourite.

Salt

Pakhuskælderen

MAP P.52, POCKET MAP F11
Nyhavn 71 ⓣ 33 43 62 14, ⓦ pakhuskaelderen.com. Mon–Sat noon–midnight.

Part of the grand *71 Nyhavn* hotel overlooking Copenhagen's harbour, this stylish gourmet restaurant features exposed pine beams and plenty of atmosphere. Continental menu specialities include *moules marinières* (95kr) or breast of poularde with basil and artichokes (230kr). Also has a great bar.

Rebel

MAP P.62, POCKET MAP E10
Store Kongensgade 52 ⓣ 33 32 32 09, ⓦ restaurantrebel.dk. Tues–Sat 5.30pm–midnight.

Compact restaurant spread over two floors serving elegant French-inspired tapas. It's especially renowned for its beef tartare, served with rhubarb, herbed mayonnaise and vinaigrette, and turbot served with escargot, lobster glaze and tarragon. 'The little rebel' meal is a great variety of flavours if you are undecided, 525kr.

Salt

MAP P.52, POCKET MAP F11
Toldbodgade 24 ⓣ 33 74 14 44, ⓦ saltrestaurant.dk. Daily noon to 4pm & 5–10pm.

Hotel Admiral's characterful restaurant has seating both in the charming wood-beamed interior and out on the waterfront. The Modern Danish food is created from traditional foundations, with a menu that changes each month. The excellent seafood menu (from 135kr) and the mouthwatering selection of Nordic cheeses (135kr) can hardly be bettered.

Taste

MAP P.52, POCKET MAP E10
Store Kongensgade 80–82 ⓣ 33 93 77 97, ⓦ tastedeli.eu. Tues–Fri 9.30am–6pm, Sat–Mon 10am–6pm.

This fabulous deli (with a few tables out front) serves gorgeous

Vespa

home-made salads, sandwiches plus a range of exquisite cakes – though as everything is of tip top quality nothing comes cheap. Try the grilled goat's cheese, beetroot and walnut sandwich, with a honey and rosemary dressing (78kr).

Vespa

MAP P.52, POCKET MAP F6
Store Kongensgade 90 ☎ 33 11 37 00, ⓦ cofoco.dk. Mon–Sat 5.30pm–midnight.
Part of the Cofoco "food empire", which follows a simple no-frills concept. What's on offer is a well-prepared four-course Italian set menu for 275kr. Restrictive perhaps, but excellent value for money.

Bars

Den Vandrette

MAP P.52, POCKET MAP F12
Havnegade 53A ☎ 72 14 82 28, ⓦ denvandrette.dk. Mon–Sat 4–11pm.
Wine cellar next to Copenhagen's newest harbour bridge, with a bare decor of brick and oak, soft lighting and a range of lesser-known biodynamic and organic wines behind the counter.

Toldboden

MAP P.52, POCKET MAP G5
Nordre Toldbod 24 ☎ 33 93 07 60, ⓦ toldboden.com. Mon–Thurs 10am–9pm, Fri 10am–midnight, Sat–Sun 9.30am–9pm.
With great views of the Inner Harbour, *Tolboden* has few rivals for the title of Copenhagen's most stunningly located bar. Come and drink here in summer months, when you can chill out on the deckchairs. As well as its bar/ clubbing profile, *Toldboden* also offers a popular weekend brunch and grill buffet.

Club

At Dolores

MAP P.32, POCKET MAP D11
Lille Kongensgade 16 ⓦ at-dolores.com. Fri–Sat 11pm–5am.
Much-hyped nightclub frequented by celebs and wannabes, the latest incarnation of the promoters behind now-defunct *Sunday Club*. Pre-register online; no under-27s.

Rosenborg and around

Christian IV's Renaissance summer palace, the Rosenborg Slot, provides a regal contrast with the crowded streets of the inner city to the east. To its west, running from Østerport station in the north to Vesterport in the south is an almost continuous string of attractive parks and gardens. Apart from being lovely places to explore, they also house a couple of significant art museums: the Statens Museum for Kunst and Hirschsprungske Samling, and the city's Botanical Gardens. It was thanks to visionary town planner Ferdinand Meldahl that the ring of ramparts and bastions encircling the city here were maintained as a green belt in 1857. The area between the ramparts and the lake later developed into sought-after residential areas and streets such as Nansensgade have a strong neighbourhood feel.

Rosenborg Slot

MAP P.62, POCKET MAP E6
4A Østervoldgade ☎ 33 15 32 86,
Ⓦ rosenborgslot.dk. Opening times vary,
check website. Castle: 115kr, 155kr
combined with Amalienborg. Gardens: free.

A Disney-esque fairy-tale palace, the **Rosenborg Slot** was originally built as a summer residence for Christian IV, a retreat from the rabble at Christiansborg. Completed in 1634, it's a grand

Rosenborg Slot

Park life

Based around the Rosenborg Slot, the beautifully manicured **Kongens Have** (King's Garden) is Copenhagen's oldest park. Visitors come to see the famous statue of Hans Christian Andersen and watch live music and puppet-theatre performances during the summer (June–Aug daily except Mon 2 & 3pm; free; ⓦmarionetteatret.dk). Stretching north from the Botanisk Have (Botanical Gardens), the undulating hills of **Østre Anlæg** are part of the old fortifications and house a number of different children's playgrounds including one in front of the National Museum of Art. **Ørstedsparken**, with its rolling hills and rampart lake, is a popular place to go in winter for skating and downhill sledging. There are also two innovative playgrounds here, one with staff at hand to show you the ropes. Come nightfall it becomes a gay hangout (in case you were wondering about the signs promoting safe sex).

red-brick Renaissance edifice decorated with spires and towers and ornate Dutch gables. The palace remained a royal residence until 1838, when it was opened to the public.

The star exhibit inside is the **crown jewels**, chief among them the Crown of the Absolute Monarch which weighs in at a hefty two kilos and sports two massive sapphires. The jewels are kept locked in the basement Treasury, behind thick steel doors. Also downstairs are the priceless wines of the Royal cellar, only cracked open at very special occasions. Before heading down here it's worth taking in Frederik III's lavish marble room with its extravagant stucco ceiling and a chess set made up of Danish and Swedish pieces (in reference to the war he lost to Karl Gustav in 1658). Another highlight of the palace is the magnificent **Long Hall** on the second floor with its gilded coronation throne, made from narwhal tusk, and three silver lions standing guard.

Botanisk Have

MAP P.62, POCKET MAP E6
Gothersgade 128 ⓦ botanik.snm.ku.dk.
Daily: April–Sept 8.30am–6pm; Oct–March 8.30am–4pm.

Relocated in 1874 from a small park behind Charlottenborg palace the **Botanisk Have** (Botanical Gardens) packs in pretty much every plant you'll find in Denmark together with several exotic species. It's a pleasant and peaceful place to wander, with its long squiggly pond clearly showing the area's previous incarnation as the city ramparts. Among the many greenhouses in the gardens, the grand Palm House overshadows them all. It was donated by brewing magnate Carl Jacobsen who was deeply involved in its design and various ingenious temperature and humidity controls. You will also find houses for cacti, orchids, alpine plants, and a new greenhouse for endangered species (check the website for their specific opening times). Guided tours are available in English; days vary, so check the website.

The Botanical Museum, part of the gardens, is currently closed. A brand new National Natural History Museum, complete with innovative underground architecture, is due to open in 2020 at the northern end of the gardens.

Statens Museum for Kunst

MAP P.62, POCKET MAP E5
Sølvgade 48–50 ☎ 33 74 84 94, ⓦ smk.

dk. Tues & Thurs–Sun 10am–6pm, Wed 10am–8pm. 120kr
Found in the southeastern corner of Østre Anlæg park, the vast **Statens Museum for Kunst** (National Museum of Art) houses the bulk of Christian II's extensive collection of European paintings and sculptures. Housed in an 1896 building by Dahlerup (see also Ny Carlsberg Glyptotek, page 26) and complemented by a modern extension in 1998, the collection is divided into European art from the fourteenth to the eighteenth century, Danish and Nordic Art from 1750 to 1900, French art from 1900–1930, and modern art from the twentieth century. Trying to see it all in one day is almost impossible. Instead, if you're interested in Danish art, head straight for the second floor where works from the so-called Golden Age – the nineteenth century – are displayed in largely chronological order. Look out especially for the beautifully lit paintings of the Skagen school – among them P.S. Krøyer and Anna Ancher. Look out too for the stark almost photographic scenes of Copenhagen in the nineteenth century by Vilhelm Hammershøi. On the second floor you'll also find work from the twentieth-century CoBrA movement (a collection of artists from Copenhagen, Brussels and Amsterdam). Contemporary international art is displayed in the museum's new extension. Recent temporary exhibits have included Matisse and Miró.

Hirschsprungske Samling
MAP P.62, POCKET MAP F5
Stockholmsgade 20 ☎ 35 42 03 36,
ⓦ hirschsprung.dk. Wed–Sun 11am–4pm. 95kr.
More manageable than the Statens Museum, the

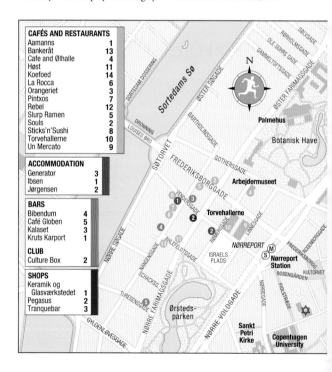

CAFÉS AND RESTAURANTS
Aamanns	1
Bankeråt	13
Cafe and Ølhalle	4
Høst	11
Koefoed	14
La Rocca	6
Orangeriet	3
Pintxos	7
Rebel	12
Slurp Ramen	5
Souls	2
Sticks'n'Sushi	8
Torvehallerne	10
Un Mercato	9

ACCOMMODATION
Generator	3
Ibsen	1
Jørgensen	2

BARS
Bibendum	4
Café Globen	5
Kalaset	3
Kruts Karport	1

CLUB
Culture Box	2

SHOPS
Keramik og Glasværkstedet	1
Pegasus	2
Tranquebar	3

Hirschsprung Collection focuses on art from the Danish Golden Age (1800–1850), donated by Heinrich Hirschsprung, a second-generation German Jew who had made his fortune in tobacco. Housed in a beautiful Neoclassical pavilion, paintings are displayed in small intimate rooms (a condition Hirschsprung set before handing over his collection to the state). As at the Staten Museum, the work of the Skagen artists P.S. Krøyer and Anna Ancher particularly stands out. Tranquil bucolic landscapes by P.C. Skovgaard and Johan Lundbye are also worth noting. More entertaining are the gossip-magazine-like paintings by Kristian Zahrtmann who depicted eighteenth-century royal scandals such as English-born Queen Caroline Mathilde's affair with court physician Johann Friedrich Struensee.

Statens Museum for Kunst

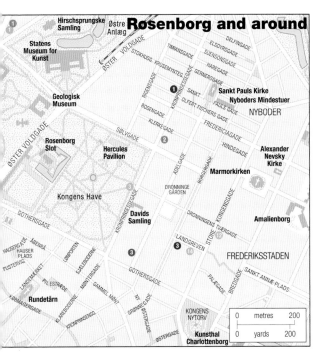

A taste of Torvehallerne

A few of Torvehallerne's best stalls are listed below and should be visited in their own right. ⓦ torvehallernekbh.dk:

Unika (stall F5) – retail outlet for cheeses usually only sold to Michelin-starred restaurants.

Grød (stall A8) – sells porridge, risotto and anything else eaten with a spoon, exclusively.

The Coffee Collective (stall C1) – the best coffee in town.

Hallernes Smørrebrød (stall F2) – great smørrebrød selected from a large display cabinet; Mikkeller on draught.

Gorms Pizza (stall G1) – freshly made pizza from a wood-fired oven.

Tapa del Torro (stall F10) – delicious home-made tapas.

Summerbird (stall A3) – chocolate made in heaven.

Arbejdermuseet

MAP P.62, POCKET MAP A10
Rømersgade 22 ⓣ 33 93 25 75,
ⓦ arbejdermuseet.dk. Daily 10am–4pm,
Wed 7pm, 90kr.
Dedicated to the Danish workers movement, **Arbejdermuseet** is housed in the group's old meeting house from 1878 and covers the cultural history of the Danish working class from 1850 onwards. Although it's probably more of interest to Danes, the historic assembly hall is worth a peek. Its tranquil bucolic decor witnessed some of the movement's most significant gatherings, not least the Socialist World Congress of 1910 which had Lenin himself in attendance (there's a Russian-made statue of him in the foyer dating from the late 1980s). The children's section, although mostly in Danish, is also popular, and often noisy, featuring doll's houses, dressing-up gear, colouring-in books and even a small pretend brewery. There's also a museum shop selling iconic workers' posters from the old Soviet Union and a basement restaurant (see page 67) knocking out traditional workers' dishes from the last century.

Davids Samling

MAP P.62, POCKET MAP D10
Kronprinsessegade 30 ⓣ 33 73 49 49,
ⓦ davidmus.dk. Tues & Thurs–Sun
10am–5pm, Wed 10am–9pm. Free.
Spread over all five floors of an eighteenth-century apartment building, the captivating **Davids Samling** comprises the remarkable collection of one C.L. David (1878–1960), a Danish lawyer who devoted his life to the acquisition of fine and applied art. It's a labyrinth of rooms, and the museum plan handed out on arrival will prove essential. The highlight without doubt is the extensive exhibition of Islamic art on the third and fourth floors. One of the most important in the West, it includes delicate Persian miniatures, striking blue Ottoman mosaics and beautifully decorated glass bowls from Egypt and Syria. David's collections of eighteenth- and nineteenth-century porcelain and furniture and twentieth-century art (look out for the evocative landscape paintings by Vilhelm Hammershøi and the extravagant French ceramics) are also impressive but don't match the heights of the Islamic finds.

Torvehallerne and Israels Plads

MAP P.62, POCKET MAP B10
Market halls: Frederiksborggade 21
ⓦ torvehallernekbh.dk. Tues–Thurs
10am–7pm, Fri 10am–8pm, Sat 10am–6pm,
Sun 11am–5pm.
The **Torvehallerne** food hall (see page 68) is Copenhagen's most

popular marketplace, attracting some 115,000 visitors a week to its 60-plus artisan stalls and restaurants. **Israels Plads** square next door, traditionally known for its flower stalls, reopened after two years of renovation, and this busy square fills with people in the summer, where its "flying carpet" architecture merges with neighbouring Ørstedsparken. The square was given its current name in 1968 in memory of Jewish persecution in Denmark during World War II.

Nyboder

MAP P.62, POCKET MAP F6.
Nyboder Mindestuer, 24 Sankt Paulsgade
☎ 50 56 49 69, ⓦ nybodersmindestuer.dk.
Sun 11am–2pm. 20kr.

The Coffee Collective, Torvehallerne

Standing out in contrast to the area's grand regal mansions, the colourful and quaint **Nyboder** district is made up of a series of rows of cute, predominantly ochre-coloured terraced houses. The area was originally built in the 1630s to provide housing for Christian IV's ever-expanding naval fleet, though most of the current buildings date from the eighteenth century – all except for a single row of houses along Sankt Paulsgade, where the

Nyboders Mindestuer (Nyboder Memorial Rooms) has been largely kept intact and functions as a museum, with tours available by appointment. Diminutive though Nyboder's houses may be, this has always been a sought-after place to live, with its own private school and hospital, and demand remains high, particularly these days priority is no longer given to military personnel.

Dining with the Danes

The "New Nordic Cuisine" scene burst onto the global stage in 2010 when Copenhagen's *Noma* (see page 73) was named the world's best restaurant. The double-act behind it, restaurateur Claus Meyer and chef René Redzepi, blazed a trail by taking inspiration from, instead of being restricted by, the limited produce of Nordic countries. Seasonal, ethically sourced ingredients (often foraged or homegrown), are prepared using methods rooted in Nordic traditions - marinated, smoked or salted for example. The Danish capital continues to garner more Michelin stars than Stockholm, Oslo and Helsinki put together, and boasts a slew of eateries headed by *Noma* protégés, such as *Relæ* (see page 95) and *Amass* (see page 75), where the Nordic kitchen can be sampled and still leave your bank balance intact. Alternatively head straight to Copenhagen Street Food (see page 75), or to Torvehallerne food market (see page 68) to shop where the chefs shop.

Shops

Keramik og Glasværkstedet

MAP P.62, POCKET MAP F6
Kronprinsessegade 43 ☏ 33 32 89 91,
ⓦ keramikogglasvaerkstedet.dk. Wed–Fri
noon to 6pm, Sat 11am–2pm.
Funky workshop-cum-gallery
selling delicate and minimalist
ceramics and glassware made
on the premises by four
independent artists.

Pegasus

MAP P.62, POCKET MAP A10
Nørre Farimagsgade 53 ☏ 33 32 56 50,
ⓦ pegasus.dk. Mon & Thurs 3.30–6.30pm.
Nerdy basement store selling a huge
selection of comics and graphic
novels (new and secondhand) from
around the globe with an especially
good selection of American comics.

Tranquebar

MAP P.62, POCKET MAP E10
Borgergade 14 ☏ 33 12 55 12,
ⓦ tranquebar.net. Mon–Fri 10am–6pm, Sat
10am–4pm.

Well-stocked book and music
shop with a vast selection of travel
literature and world music (and,
of course, a good range of Rough
Guides). The bookstore café sells
lunch platters (noon–3pm) from
Koefoed (see opposite), up the road.

Cafés and restaurants

Aamanns

MAP P.62, POCKET MAP E5
Øster Farimagsgade 10–12 ☏ 20 80 52 01,
ⓦ aamanns.dk. Restaurant: Mon–Fri noon
to 4pm, Sat–Sun noon–4.30pm. Deli: Mon–
Sun 11am–8pm.
This stylish ode to traditional Danish
open sandwiches makes hands-down
the city's best smørrebrød. Head chef
Adam Aamanns ensures everything
is free range and sourced from local
Danish farmers (four-course menu
345kr). It's perfect for a visit with
children, too, who love the bite-sized
portions. You can either eat in or
take away in smart little picnic-
friendly boxes.

Aamanns

Bankeråt

MAP P.62, POCKET MAP A10
Ahlefeldtsgade 27–29 ☎ 33 93 69 88,
🖥 bankeraat.dk. Mon–Fri 9.30am–4pm, Sat
10.30am–midnight & Sun 10.30am–8pm.
Oldie but goodie Nansensgade
café which is just as popular now
as when it opened in the 80s with
its largely unchanged quirky decor.
Its signature breakfast/brunch
Morgenkomplex comes in lots of
different variations including "Full
Engelsk". Turns into a popular bar
come evening.

Cafe and Ølhalle

MAP P.62, POCKET MAP B10
Rømersgade 22 ☎ 33 33 00 18,
🖥 cafeogoelhalle.dk. Mon–Thurs
11am–5pm, Fri–Sat 11am–5pm.
You may find the traditional
nineteenth-century worker's fare
served here a little heavy, but it is
authentic and very tasty. Known
for their natural ingredients
and attention to detail, try the
popular buffet which serves up
a variety of meat and cheese
for you to create your own
sandwich (199kr).

Høst

MAP P.62, POCKET MAP A10
Nørre Farimagsgade 41 ☎ 89 93 84 09,
🖥 cofoco.dk Mon–Sun 5.30pm–midnight.
The word Høst means harvest in
Danish, so it's no surprise this
award-winning restaurant's dishes
are based around seasonal Nordic
ingredients. Housed in a typical
Copenhagen building, the interior
is relaxed and stylish with exposed
brick walls and Danish furniture.
You can go for a three or five course
menu (350kr/450kr) with meals
such as baked cod with tomatoes or
fried Norwegian lobster.

Koefoed

MAP P.62, POCKET MAP E10
Landgreven 3 ☎ 56 48 22 24, 🖥 restaurant-
koefoed.dk. Tues–Sat noon–3pm &
5.30–10pm.
Elegant *Koefoed* is an ode to the
gourmet island of Bornholm,
famous for its slow-food ethos and
quality produce. The lunchtime
smørrebrød (from 95kr) has
won awards, while the dinner
menu starts at 195kr for a main
(Bornholmer rooster or cod with
oysters, for example). Eat in the
atmospheric, vaulted, stone-
walled interior or outside on
streetside tables.

La Rocca

MAP P.62, POCKET MAP A10
Vendersgade 23–25 ☎ 33 12 66 55,
🖥 larocca.dk. Daily noon–10.30pm.
Classical Italian restaurant at *Ibsens
Hotel*, offering refined Italian
dining such as a fine mixed seafood
grill (249kr) and a couple of good
pizzas, too.

Orangeriet

MAP P.62, POCKET MAP D10
Kronprinsessegade 13 ☎ 33 11 13 07,
🖥 restaurant-orangeriet.dk. Mon–Sat
11.30am–3pm & 6–10pm, Sun noon–4pm.
Atmospheric glass-encased café-
restaurant located along the western
wall of Kongens Have, with great
views of the gardens, serving
excellent smørrebrød for lunch and
more substantial meals for dinner
starting at 210kr for fried mullet
with escabeche, spinach, spring
cabbage and sauce made with
grilled clams.

Pintxos

MAP P.62, POCKET MAP A10
Nansensgade 63 ☎ 33 93 66 55,
🖥 pintxostapas.dk. Daily 5–11pm.
Genuine Spanish restaurant with
genuine Spanish waiters, and
tapas galore (from 49kr) in a
romantic courtyard.

Slurp Ramen

MAP P.62, POCKET MAP A10
Nansensgade 90 ☎ 53 70 80 83,
🖥 slurpramen.dk. Tues 5–10pm, Wed–Sun
noon–2.30pm & 5–10pm.
Little but scrumptious ramen joint.
Its small menu features both meat
and veggie options; one dish will
set you back 140kr.

Souls

MAP P.62, POCKET MAP B10
Nørre Farimagsgade 63 6 ⓘ 33 36 33
30, ⓦ 33 30 01 50. Mon–Wed & Sun
9am–9.30pm, Thurs 9am–10pm, Fri & Sat
9am–10.30pm.

Priding itself on a green eco-friendly and vegan menu, *Souls* want to offer their food to people who are conscious of what they put in their body and their eco-footprint on the planet. They serve wonderful vegan dishes such as the Soul Burger (110kr) or Wasabi Caesar Salad (128kr).

Sticks'n'sushi

MAP P.62, POCKET MAP A10
Nansensgade 59 ⓘ 33 11 14 07, ⓦ sushi.
dk. Sun–Wed 10am–11pm, Thurs & Sat
10am–11.30pm.

Copenhagen's original purveyors of raw fish to the masses. Starting out some twenty years ago, they now have branches across the city (and in London). They can still make a mean sushi and also specialize in yakitori sticks (marinated skewers

La Rocca

of meat and fish) as well as an outstanding array of salads, best of which is the scrumptious fish-bowl salad (149kr).

Torvehallerne

MAP P.62, POCKET MAP B10
Frederiksborggade 21 ⓦ torvehallernekbh.
dk. Mon–Thurs 10am–7pm, Fri 10am–8pm,
Sat 10am–6pm, Sun 11am–5pm. Coffee
and freshly baked bread available Mon–Sat
from 8am, Sun from 9am. Restaurants and
takeaways stay open an hour later than
the market.

Denmark's biggest and best food market. It's split into two long open-sided halls, one featuring meat, cheese and fish and a non-smelly section where you'll find chocolate, bread and the like. In between are plenty of outdoor benches at which to eat. A great way to explore Torvehallerne is to join the city's new Food Tours (see page 125).

Un Mercato

MAP P.62, POCKET MAP B10
Torvehallerne, Frederiksborggade 19.
ⓦ Unmercato.dk Mon–Thurs 10am–11pm,
Fri–Sat 10am–4pm, Sun 10am–10pm.

No-nonsense Italian rotisserie on the first floor of Torvehallerne, run by the people behind *Cofoco* restaurants. The lunchtime flame-grilled chicken or porchetta sandwiches (65kr) are mouthwatering – even just writing about them.

Bars

Bibendum

MAP P.62, POCKET MAP A10
Nansensgade 45 ⓘ 33 33 07 74,
ⓦ bibendum.dk. Mon–Sat 4pm–midnight.

Small cosy basement wine bar with a huge selection of wine, all of which are sold by the glass as well as by the bottle. Also good nibbles (from 85kr) to soak up the alcohol such as cheese and charcuterie platters and a delicious fish soup.

Kalaset

Café Globen

MAP P.62, POCKET MAP A11
Turesensgade 2b ☎ 33 93 00 77,
Ⓦ cafegloben.dk. Mon–Thurs 5–10pm, Fri
5pm–1am.
Laidback travellers' haunt halfway
between a club and a café with lots
of guidebooks lying around and
people keen to talk about their
latest adventures. Selling a good
range of brews from home and
abroad, they don't mind if you
bring your own food and eat at
their tables.

Kalaset

MAP P.62, POCKET MAP A10
Vendersgade 16 ☎ 33 33 00 35, Ⓦ kalaset.
dk. Mon–Thurs 10am–midnight, Fri & Sat
10am–2am, Sun 10am–11pm.
Quirky shabby-chic basement
café which spills out onto the
pavement during summer when
it's an excellent spot to enjoy the
sunshine while sipping a cool
drink. During weekends a DJ gets
the party going.

Kruts Karport

MAP P.62, POCKET MAP E5
Øster Farimagsgade 12 ☎ 35 26 86 38,
Ⓦ kruts.dk. Mon–Thurs 2pm–midnight, Fri
& Sat 2pm–2am, Sun 2–9pm.
Copenhagen's first French-style
café, *Kruts Karport* stocks the city's
largest selection of whisky, and
is one of the few places you can
order an absinthe. That said, the
selection of foreign draught beer is
not bad either.

Club

Culture Box

MAP P.62, POCKET MAP F6
Kronprinsessegade 54 ☎ 33 32 50 50,
Ⓦ culture-box.com. Fri & Sat 11pm–8am.
Spread over two floors, with a
Berlin-style industrial decor, this
popular bar-club keeps going until
the wee hours of the morning.
Revellers tend to get the party
started first at *The White Box*
cocktail bar next door.

Christianshavn and Holmen

With its tight network of narrow canals and cobbled streets, Christianshavn – sometimes known as Little Amsterdam – is one of the city's most charming areas. Water is omnipresent, perhaps not surprising given that the island was constructed from reclaimed land in the sixteenth century to form a defensive arc around the city. For the most part the attractions here are low-key, though Christianshavn's principal source of tourist intrigue – the unique "Freetown" of Christiania, home to one of the world's most famous alternative communities – pulls in almost a million visitors a year. To the north, former naval base Holmen and its neighbouring islands have been re-energized after decades of disuse with post-industrial developments like the national opera house and an old shipyard, B&W Hallerne, that was rebuilt to host 2014's Eurovision Song Contest. To the south, Islands Brygge quay stretches along the harbourfront of Amager, and is worth visiting for its waterside park and lively cultural centre.

Christianshavns Kanal

MAP P.72, POCKET MAP E14–F14

Lined on both sides by cobbled streets and colourful merchant's houses, the tranquil **Christianshavns Kanal** originally provided the main way of accessing the island. This picturesque area is redolent of old Amsterdam, and indeed was designed by a Dutch architect, Johan Semp, who was commissioned in the early seventeenth century by Christian IV to plan the district.

Then as now, Christianshavn's main square, **Christianshavn Torv**, was the focal point of public transport to the island – today there's a metro station (underground) and constant flow of buses, as well as a canal-boat stop. A notable exception to the imposing historic buildings around the square is the modernist **Lagkagehuset** (Layercake House) at Torvegade

45. It created riotous debate when it was built in 1931 as it was felt it didn't blend in to its historic surroundings but today is deemed a national treasure.

Christians Kirke

MAP P.72, POCKET MAP E14
Strandgade 1 ⓦ christianskirke.dk. **Tues–Fri 11am–5pm.**

Surrounded by modern offices and apartments, Eigtved's Rococo **Christians Kirke** (1759) looks oddly out of place. It was originally built for the city's German congregation and still functions as a church, though its theatre-like interior makes it an excellent music venue.

Vor Frelserskirke

MAP P.72, POCKET MAP F13
Skt Annæ Gade 29 ☎ 32 54 68 83, ⓦ vorfrelserskirke.dk. **Church: daily 11am–3.30pm; free. Tower: June to mid-Sept daily 10am–7pm; mid-Sept to May daily 10am–4pm (Sun opens at 10.30am); 35kr.**

Capped by an iconic church tower, its soaring spire wrapped in a gilded spiral external staircase which culminates in a globe carrying a flag-waving Jesus, **Vor Frelserskirke** (Our Saviour's Church) is an unmissable feature of the Christianshavn skyline. Constructed in the late 1600s, the church owes its opulence to Christian V, whose status as Denmark's first absolute monarch is underlined by some lavish Baroque flourishes. Inside, look out especially for the two stucco elephants holding up the gigantic three-storey organ, though the real highlight is the ascent of the **tower**, accessed by a separate entrance. There are 400 steps to the top, 150 of which are external – quite a challenge on a busy summer's day – but the stupendous views across the city are ample reward.

Christiania

MAP P.72, POCKET MAP G8
Main entrance on Prinsessegade.
Infocaféen daily noon–6pm. Guided tours (starting at the main entrance) Sat & Sun 3pm; 40kr.

A self-proclaimed autonomous enclave with its own governance and rules, **Freetown Christiania** is Copenhagen's main alternative claim to fame. Ever since 1971, when a group of homeless Copenhageners first occupied the disued Bådsmandsstræde army barracks, Christiania has attracted controversy, its very existence perennially threatened (see page 73). Today, thanks in no small part to its open cannabis trade, it's one of the city's most visited tourist attractions. Despite its dishevelled look and whacked-out feel, it's a remarkable place. Egalitarian, creative and ecologically minded, the ideals of its thousand-or-so residents have resulted in some truly unique self-built homes, imaginative businesses, and a host of artistic venues.

Extending for around 1km along the bastions that straddle Christian IV's picturesque defensive moat, there is quite a lot of Christiania to see, and the best way to experience it is either to join one of the immensely

Mural, Christiania

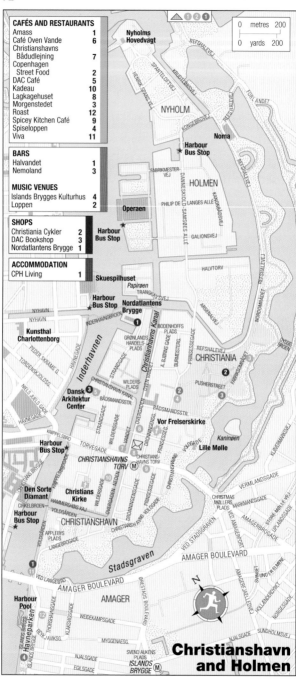

CAFÉS AND RESTAURANTS

Amass	1
Café Oven Vande	6
Christianshavns Bådudlejning	7
Copenhagen Street Food	2
DAC Café	5
Kadeau	10
Lagkagehuset	8
Morgenstedet	3
Roast	12
Spicey Kitchen Café	9
Spiseloppen	4
Viva	11

BARS

Halvandet	1
Nemoland	3

MUSIC VENUES

Islands Brygges Kulturhus	4
Loppen	2

SHOPS

Christiania Cykler	2
DAC Bookshop	3
Nordatlantens Brygge	1

ACCOMMODATION

CPH Living	1

Christianshavn and Holmen

Christiania: reinventing itself to survive

Since its inception half a century ago, residents have struggled to defend Christiania's existence. Clashes over the residents' occupation (for free) of prime city real estate, past non-payment of taxes, with police over the drug trade and finally, the government's plans for redevelopment, forced temporary closure in 2011. Residents managed to broker a remarkable deal with the government, however, to buy back the buildings at sub-market rates (still 76 million kroner), and to pay annual rent of 6 million kroner for the rest, issuing so-called People's Shares (Ⓦ christianiafolkeaktie.dk) as a way for outside supporters to fund its survival. In 2018, the community was surprised to see world-acclaimed restaurant *Noma* (2500kr for its twenty-course extravaganza), move to an ex-military warehouse on a scrappy plot beside Christiania.

informative (if inevitably one-sided) guided tours, or buy a copy of the *Christiania Guide* (20kr) from the Infocaféen, in the **Loppebygningen** building to the left of the main entrance. Housed within the same building, a former artillery magazine, are the **Gallopperiet** art gallery (Ⓦ gallopperiet.dk), *Spiseloppen* restaurant (see page 76) and Loppen music venue (see page 77).

Continuing along the main artery, you reach **Carl Madsens Plads**, lined with stalls selling knick-knacks and fast food, which marks the beginning of **Pusherstreet** – impossible to miss from its unmistakeable aroma. Lining the street are rows of well-stocked shacks selling everything from pre-rolled joints to smoking paraphernalia. A couple of basic rules apply on Pusherstreet: don't run (or the stallholders will think there's a police raid) and don't take photos. Also remember that the use of hash is still a criminal offence in Denmark.

Following the edge of the moat around from *Nemoland* (see page 77) leads you into the quieter, greener and more residential area. Here you will find some of Christiania's most ingenious alternative dwellings. A pedestrian bridge crosses the moat at the next bastion, or you can continue along past four bastions to the public road at the end, and follow the moat path back on the opposite side.

Dansk Arkitektur Center

MAP P.72, POCKET MAP F13
Strandgade 27B ☎ 32 57 19 30, Ⓦ dac.dk.
Mon-Sun 10am–6pm & Thurs 10am–9pm.
110kr. Architectural tours available, check website for times.

Housed in a beautifully restored warehouse building on the waterfront next to the former naval dry dock (the most advanced of its kind when constructed in the sixteenth century), the **Danish Architecture Centre** hosts changing exhibitions of new Danish and international architecture, has a well-stocked bookshop and a first-floor café with perhaps the best views in town (see page 75).

In summer the centre organizes weekly **tours** on foot or by bike to an area of Copenhagen of particular interest to fans of new architecture – typically to Ørestaden, Holmen or along the harbourfront (tours usually start at

CHRISTIANSHAVN AND HOLMEN

the tourist information office on Vesterbrogade; book on Ⓦ dac.dk).

Operaen

MAP P.72, POCKET MAP G6

Holmen ⓘ 33 69 69 69, Ⓦ operaen.dk.
Tours most Sat & Sun; 100kr. Harbour Bus.

Occupying a prominent position on the compact island of Holmen diametrically across the water from the Marmorkirken, the Henning Larsen-designed **Operaen** (Opera House) is visible from almost any point along the harbour. It's a striking building, surmounted by an enormous flat roof that delicately overhangs the water's edge, while the no-expense-spared interior features gigantic outlandish lighting globes, designed by Danish-Icelandic artist Oluf Eliasson, in the foyer; note too the Jura sandstone walls inset with masses of tiny fossils. To gain access, though, you'll need either to see a performance (doors open 2hr beforehand) or join a guided tour.

Islands Brygge

MAP P.72, POCKET MAP F9

Just south of Christianshavn, on the island of Amager, the Islands Brygge development is fast becoming one of the city's most happening areas. Much of this former industrial harbour strip has been converted into a waterfront park, the **Havneparken** – popular with people from all walks of life, from parents with prams to parkour enthusiasts – with cultural activity focused around the Islands Brygges Kulturhus (see page 77). Best of all, however, is the innovative, council-run **harbour pool** (May–Sept Mon–Fri 7am–7pm, Sat & Sun 9am–7pm; free), the perfect place to cool off in the summer.

The quayside walkway extends all the way south to the bicycle and pedestrian bridge, officially the **Bryggebroen** ("Quay bridge"), which gives access to Fisketorvet and Vesterbro.

Operaen

Shops

Christiania Cykler

MAP P.72, POCKET MAP G8
Mælkeven 83A, Christiania ☎ 32 54 87 48,
ⓦ christianiabikes.dk. Mon–Tues & Thurs–
Fri 9am–5.30pm, Wed 10am–5.30pm, Sat
11am–3pm.
Classic, sturdy and super-cool,
Christiania Bikes' hand-crafted
three-wheel cargo cycles are one
of the city's icons. Prices start at
10,100kr.

DAC Bookshop

MAP P.72, POCKET MAP F13
Strandgade 27B ☎ 32 57 19 30, ⓦ dac.dk.
Mon–Fri 10am–6pm, Wed till 9pm, Sat &
Sun 10am–5pm.
The Danish Architecture Centre's
attractive bookshop stocks just
about every title on modern
architecture you could ever wish for.

Nordatlantens Brygge

MAP P.72, POCKET MAP G7
Strandgade 91 ☎ 32 83 37 00, ⓦ bryggen.
dk. Mon–Fri 10am–5pm, Sat & Sun
noon–5pm. Entry (also for shop) 40kr.
Housed in an enormous
eighteenth-century warehouse,
Nordatlantens Brygge promotes
artistic and cultural links between
Denmark, Greenland, Iceland
and the Faroe Islands. A small
store at the back sells regional
music and crafts such as Icelandic
knitwear and sealskin slippers
from Greenland.

Cafés and restaurants

Amass

MAP P.72, POCKET MAP H5
Refshalevej 153 ☎ 43 58 43 30,
ⓦ amassrestaurant.com. Dinner: Tues–
Sat 6pm–midnight; Lunch: Fri & Sat
noon–3.30pm.
Amass' opening on industrial
Refshaleøen island in 2013
created quite a stir: owner and

head chef, Matthew Orlando is
formerly of *Noma*, and *Amass* is
similarly focused on local produce
but dining is simpler here, with
a "drop-in" table and communal
eating encouraged.

Café Oven Vande

MAP P.72, POCKET MAP F13
Overgaden Oven Vandet 44 ☎ 32 95 96
02, ⓦ cafeovenvande.dk. Daily 10am–
midnight.
With tables and chairs spilling
out onto the pavement, this
Christianshavn institution is a
fine place to enjoy an excellent
lunchtime smørrebrød platter
(159kr) by the canal. Catching the
sunset, it's also hugely popular in
the evening when there's a French-
inspired menu.

Christianshavns Bådudlejning

MAP P.72, POCKET MAP F14
Overgaden Neden Vandet 29 ☎ 32 96 53 53,
ⓦ baadudlejningen.dk. Daily 10am–10pm
(evening restaurant is open in summer
months only).
Formerly a boat rental point, this
partially covered floating pontoon,
moored at the Torvegade bridge, is
now a trendy lunch spot, serving
a few smørrebrød options (from
115kr), a range of colourful seafood
salads, plus cold-cut meat platters.
Open for dinner, too.

Copenhagen Street Food

MAP P.72, POCKET MAP H6
Refshalevej 167 ☎ 33 93 07 60, ⓦ reffen.
dk. Sun–Thurs noon–8pm, Fri & Sat
noon–9pm.
This food market has a more casual
feel than Torvehallerne, where
edible goodies from all around the
world are sold from the waterfront
food trucks, most of it organic and
sustainable.

DAC Café

MAP P.72, POCKET MAP F12
Strandgade 27B ☎ 32 57 19 30, ⓦ dac.dk.
Mon–Fri 11am–5pm, Wed 11am–9pm, Sat
& Sun 10am–5pm.

Apart from its wonderful panoramic views DAC's first-floor café is especially popular for the elaborate all-day weekend brunch (175kr), which includes home-made gravlax and waffles.

Kadeau

MAP P.72, POCKET MAP E14
Wildersgade 10B ☎ 33 25 22 23, ⓦ kadeau.
dk. Tues–Fri 6.30pm–midnight, Sat noon–4pm & 6.30pm–midnight.
Inspired by the Baltic isle of Bornholm – in both food and the art on display – *Kadeau* has two Michelin stars for good reason. Its inventive dishes include locally sourced octopus, beetroot and pork belly, as well as indigenous grains and berries. The "Bornholmerbank" blowout menu of twenty small servings costs 1300kr.

Lagkagehuset

MAP P.72, POCKET MAP F14
Torvegade 45 ☎ 32 57 36 07,
ⓦ lagkagehuset.dk. Daily 6am–7pm.
The original *Lagkagehuset* (there are now branches across the city), "Layercake House" (see page 70) is

Amass

an exceptional bakery-cum-patisserie serving beautiful pastries (from 30kr).

Morgenstedet

MAP P.72, POCKET MAP H8
Fabriksområdet 134, Christiania
ⓦ morgenstedet.dk. Tues–Sun noon–9pm.
Small, welcoming vegetarian place set in a cute little cottage that once belonged to the army, with tables outside in a peaceful garden. Inexpensive organic food includes a hot meal of the day, such as bean stew or potato gratin (80kr), and a selection of salads (30kr).

Roast

MAP P.72, POCKET MAP F8
Vestmannagade 4 ☎ 32 96 02 20, ⓦ roast.
com. Mon–Fri 7.30am–5pm, Sat–Sun 10am–4pm.
One of the city's most celebrated coffee spots, the staff really know their beans and the delicious-smelling roastery is on-site.

Spicey Kitchen Café

MAP P.72, POCKET MAP F14
Torvegade 56 ☎ 32 95 28 29. Daily 5pm–10pm.
Chaotic, always busy Middle Eastern café dishing up delicious and excellent-value South Asian and Middle Eastern meals – mainly curries and kebabs, with at least one vegetarian option. Prices start at 75kr for a main course.

Spiseloppen

MAP P.72, POCKET MAP G8
Prinsessegade 1, Christiania ☎ 32 57 95 58,
ⓦ spiseloppen.dk. Tues–Sat 5–10.30pm.
Considering the ramshackle staircase leading up to it, the high quality of the cuisine offered by this rustic Christiania collective comes as quite a surprise. The global reach of the menu reflects the wide origins of its chefs.

Viva

MAP P.72, POCKET MAP D14
Langebrogade Kaj 570 ☎ 27 25 05 05,
ⓦ restaurantviva.dk. Mon, Tues,Sun noon–4pm, Wed–Sat 11.30am–10pm.

Kadeau

This small and intimate boat restaurant, moored next to Langebro bridge, serves up an exquisite gourmet six-course tasting menu (400kr) as well as picnic baskets to go, plus wine menu (300kr). Don't miss a preprandial cocktail or *digestif* on the rooftop deck for a magical view of the city lights reflecting in the water.

Bars

Halvandet

MAP P.72, POCKET MAP H4
Refshalevej 325 ☎ 70 27 02 96,
🌐 halvandet.dk. Opening times vary, check their Facebook for details.
Located on a disused industrial pier on Holmen, this unusual beach bar is decked out with mattresses (rented for sun-lounging during the daytime), while things get livelier in the evening. Nibbles and light meals are available in the daytime. Best reached via harbour bus or canal boat.

Nemoland

MAP P.72, POCKET MAP G8
Christiania ☎ 32 95 89 31, 🌐 nemoland. dk. Sun–Thurs 11am–midnight, Fri–Sat 11am–3am.
This lively café-bar with a large outdoor space is a popular place for visitors to sample purchases from Pusherstreet undisturbed. There are free gigs on a rickety stage outside on summer Sundays, featuring well-known Danish artists and lesser-known international acts.

Music venues

Islands Brygges Kulturhus

MAP P.72, POCKET MAP E9
Islands Brygge 18 ☎ 33 66 47 00,
🌐 kulturhusetislandsbrygge.kk.dk. Mon–Fri 8am–10pm, Sat–Sun 10am–10pm.
The waterfront Islands Brygges Kulturhus puts on a packed programme of gigs, activities (Latin dance on Tuesdays, for example) and film nights. There's also a café-bar-restaurant with a large water-facing terrace out front.

Loppen

MAP P.72, POCKET MAP G8
Christiania ☎ 32 57 84 22, 🌐 loppen.dk.
Gigs most days of the week from 8.30/9pm, see website for details.
On the first floor of the warehouse that also houses *Spiseloppen* and the Infocaféen this usually tightly packed venue hosts superb live gigs five nights a week. Music ranges from Danish folk to hard-core punk, with admission 50–200kr.

Vesterbro and Frederiksberg

The two neighbouring districts of Vesterbro and Frederiksberg couldn't be more contrasting. Vesterbro was until recently a solidly working-class area. Urban regeneration projects over the past fifteen years have smartened it up, inflating the value of property, and attracting more affluent residents. They have also brought with them a slew of edgy art galleries, restaurants and bars such as those in the über-trendy, newly converted Kødbyen meat-packing area. Conservative Frederiksberg combines elegant tree-lined avenues, beautiful parks and grand villas – a stroll down Frederiksberg Allé to the romantic seventeenth-century Frederiksberg Have (gardens) and palace gives a flavour of its well-heeled opulence. The quaint little street of Værnedamsvej links the two districts with some superb places to eat and drink, exclusive shops and a neighbourly, outgoing feel.

Vesterbrogade and Istedgade

MAP P.80, POCKET MAP B8–E8

As one of the main arteries leading into the city, **Vesterbrogade** has been lined with restaurants and inns since the sixteenth century. Today, it offers access to the hugely popular nightlife of Kødbyen, and retains a bohemian atmosphere thanks to the large number of artists

Værnedamsvej

The Carlsberg Quarter

The site of the old Carlsberg Brewery has seen a transformation of epic proportions since the beer giant moved production to Jutland in 2006. After a long period of public consultation, in 2013 an inspired develpment plan was announced: to turn the site into a vibrant cultural and residential quarter, **Carlsberg Byen** ("Carlsberg City"). Now, former brewery buildings complete with original giant copper kettles, are fashionable events spaces. New-builds have sprung up to house chic apartments, restaurants, offices and shops. The first hotel to open, spread across two industrial buildings, was **Hotel Ottilia** (ⓦ brochner-hotels.com/hotel-ottilia) - think Danish furniture set against a backdrop of twenty-metre-high ceilings. Other points of interest include **Dansehallerne** (ⓦ dansehallerne.dk), a modern-dance performance venue at **Tap E, Encoded** (ⓦ encoded.dk) a Danish handcrafted furniture and interior design store. You could easily spend a half-day exploring the complex. Landmark sights include the iconic **Elephant Gate**, the glorious winding Lotus Chimney, the Lime Tower lighthouse and the Star Gate, the original main entrance to the brewery. Many of Carlsberg's luscious green spaces have also been opened up to the public J.C. Jacobsen's delightfully tranquil garden, laid out in 1848.

and musicians who still live here. Running roughly parallel, **Istedgade** is all that is left of the city's once infamous red-light district which flourished after the legalization of pornography in the 1960s. Today a handful of hookers and the occasional porn shop near Central Station is all that remains.

Musikmuseet

MAP P.80, POCKET MAP C6
Rosenørns Alle 22 ☏ 33 13 44 11, ⓦ natmus.dk/museerne/musikmuseet. Tues–Sun 10am–4pm. Adult 70kr (children free), family ticket 50kr.

After years in storage, the many bizarre exhibits of the Danish museum of music have finally re-emerged in the highly appropriate setting of DR's former radio house, a modernist building designed by acclaimed architect Vilhelm Lauritzen in 1954, close to the Forum exhibition hall and metro station. The instruments on display, which include an amoeba-shaped

violin and giraffe piano, come from all four corners of the globe and date back as far as the 1500s; there is also the "klang room", a specially soundproofed room where children can play their hearts out without disturbing the neighbours.

Tycho Brahe Planetarium

MAP P.80, POCKET MAP D8
Gammel Kongevej 10 ☏ 33 12 12 24, ⓦ planetariet.dk. Mon noon–8pm, Tues–Sun 9am–8pm. Adults/children under 12 160kr/99kr including IMAX film, 89kr/64kr without.

Housed in a massive and unmissable yellow-brick cylinder at the foot of Sankt Jørgens lake, the city's **planetarium** is named after sixteenth-century Danish astronomer Tycho Brahe. For many visitors – especially the local schoolkids who overrun the place during the week – the main attraction is the enormous 3D IMAX screen in the planetarium's central Space Theatre, which shows science and nature films.

VESTERBRO AND FREDERIKSBERG

Kødbyen

MAP P.80, POCKET MAP D9

Once Copenhagen's former meat-packing district, **Kødbyen** is now one of the trendiest areas in the city. It encompasses cutting-edge galleries and arty cocktail bars, rustic-chic restaurants and grungy nightclubs, with a vibe that changes through the day. Until noon the feel is cold industrial, with life emanating only from the few remaining food-processing plants. After lunch, the galleries begin to open and a colourful, trendsetting crowd moves in. Come evening the restaurants pack out with diners and then partygoers who continue the evening milling from bar to bar, and later on into the nightclubs.

Kødbyen's earliest buildings – the eastern, "brown" part of the site – date back to the late nineteenth century when the city's slaughterhouses were focused on one site in a bid to improve hygiene. The original indoor cattle market has now been converted into the **Øksnehallen** exhibition centre, an interesting building with a vast vaulted ceiling that hosts regular photography exhibitions as well as trade fairs for food and fashion, most of them open to the public. In the 1930s the district was extended with the so-called "white" section to the west, whose functionalist blue-and-white-tile-covered buildings are now protected as an industrial monument.

Carlsberg Visitor Centre

MAP P.80, POCKET MAP B9
Gamle Carlsbergvej 11 ☏ 33 27 12 82, Wvisitcarlsberg.dk. Daily 10am–5pm (closed for renovations, set to reopen in 2020). 85kr.

Carlsberg's slick visitor centre takes you through the history of the brewery and provides an insight

Vesterbro and Frederiksberg

SHOPS
Designer Zoo — 4
Donn Ya Doll — 1
Meyers Deli — 5
Samsøe og Samsøe — 2
SummerBird — 3

BARS
Bang & Jensen — 7
Curfew — 3
Falernum — 2
Märkbar — 4
Mesteren & Lærlingen — 9
Mikkeller — 5
Salon 39 — 1
Vinbaren Vesterbro Torv — 6

MUSIC VENUE
Vega — 8

CAFÉS AND RESTAURANTS
Anarki — 1
Bento — 11
Café Viggo — 2
Cofoco — 10
Famo — 8
Frk. Barners Kælder — 9
Granola — 7
Hansens Gamle Familiehave — 7
Kødbyens Fiskebar — 14
Lê Lê Nhà Hang — 6
Mad & Kaffe — 16
Madklubben Vesterbro — 5
Mother — 13
Paté Paté — 12
Riccos Kaffebar — 15
Spuntino — 4
Sticks'n'Sushi — 17

into the interlinked history of Danes and beer. Highlights include the world's largest collection of beer bottles (over 20,000) and a wonderful assortment of old advertising campaigns. Although it lacks the noise and excitement of a large working brewery, you do get the opportunity to sample (alongside regular Carlsberg) some interesting beers from the on-site microbrewery, the **Jacobsen Brewhouse**, at the end of your visit.

Frederiksberg Have and Slot

MAP P.80, POCKET MAP A8
Roskildevej Ⓦ kongeligeslotte.dk. Gardens: 7am–sunset; free. Palace: guided tours Jan–June & Aug–Nov last Sat of the month 11am & 1pm; 50kr.

One of the city's most beautiful and romantic spots, **Frederiksberg Have** was originally laid out in the late seventeenth century as gardens for

Elephant Gate, Carlsberg Quarter

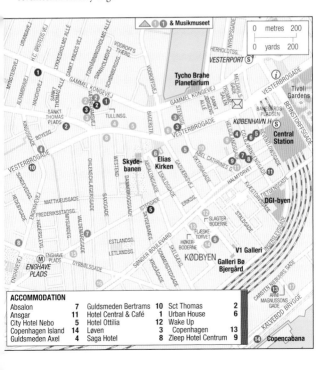

ACCOMMODATION

Absalon	7	Guldsmeden Bertrams	10
Ansgar	11	Hotel Central & Café	1
City Hotel Nebo	5	Hotel Ottilia	12
Copenhagen Island	14	Løven	3
Guldsmeden Axel	4	Saga Hotel	8

Sct Thomas	2
Urban House	6
Wake Up Copenhagen	13
Zleep Hotel Centrum	9

Zoologisk Have

the recently completed royal palace. The gardens' Baroque formality was remodelled in the English landscape style a century later, with winding paths weaving across undulating lawns, boating canals and numerous follies hidden among the trees. The park can be accessed from all sides, but arriving from the *slot* gives you the best overview of its layout. Hugely popular for picnicking and lounging, the gardens also host music and theatre performances in summer (check the website for details).

Frederiksberg Slot itself, built in Baroque style, was the royal family's main summer residence until the mid-1800s, and now houses the Danish Officers Academy – it's therefore off-limits except for the infrequent guided tours. The interior is awash with intricate stuccowork and bold and colourful ceiling paintings; grandest of all is the elaborately decorated chapel, which you may find a little over the top.

Zoologisk Have

MAP P.80, POCKET MAP A8
Roskildevej 32 ☎ 72 20 02 00, ⓦ zoo.dk.
Open from 10am; closing times vary (check website). 195kr, children under 12 105kr.
Founded in 1859, Copenhagen's **zoological gardens** encompass everything you'd expect from a zoo with over 2500 caged animals from around the globe. Aside from the wooden 44m observation tower (1905), two recently added structures stand out: Foster & Partners' etched-glass-domed **Elephant House**, complete with underfloor heating, and Danish architects Dall & Lindhardsen's **Hippo House**, where you can watch the animals frolic underwater. Both are easily visible from neighbouring parks (Frederiksberg Have for the elephants and Søndermarken for the hippos), so – should you wish – you can avoid forking out the entrance fee to view them.

Shops

Designer Zoo

MAP P.80, POCKET MAP B8

Vesterbrogade 137 ☎ 51 51 54 82, Ⓦ **designerzoo.dk. Mon–Thurs 10am–5.30pm, Fri 10am–7pm, Sat 10am–3pm.**
Welcoming store run by eight designers selling own-made furniture, jewellery, knitwear, pottery and glass. A great place for that elusive Christmas gift.

Donn Ya Doll

MAP P.80, POCKET MAP D8

Istedgade 55 ☎ 33 22 66 35, Ⓦ **donnyadoll. dk. Mon–Fri 11am–6pm, Sat 10am–4pm.**
This chaotic clothes shop sells sustainably produced clothes, from bamboo underwear to soya shirts including items made by top Danish designers such as Stig P and Eco Nord.

Meyers Deli

MAP P.80, POCKET MAP C7

Gammel Kongevej 107 ☎ 33 25 45 95, Ⓦ **meyersmad.dk. Daily 7am–8pm.**
The original branch of what is now a chain, selling delicious home-made bread as well as delicacies like honey-cured ham, home-made pâtés, pickles and chutneys, and freshly pressed apple juice.

Samsøe og Samsøe

MAP P.80, POCKET MAP C8

Værnedamsvej 12 ☎ 35 28 51 02, Ⓦ **samsoe. com. Mon–Thurs 10am–6pm, Fri 10am–7pm, Sat 10am–4pm, Sun 11am–4pm.**
Cool own-brand designer wear for men and women, plus a few items from other labels. They're known for their simple, loose-fitting style and punchy colours.

SummerBird

MAP P.80, POCKET MAP C8

Værnedamsvej 9 ☎ 33 25 25 50, Ⓦ **summerbird.dk. Mon–Fri 11am–6pm, Sat 10am–3pm.**
Dinky little chocolatier selling arguably the world's best chocolate. Try the otherworldly *flødeboller*

(cream buns) – fluffy, chocolate-coated marshmallow treats.

Cafés and restaurants

Anarki

MAP P.80, POCKET MAP D7

Vodroffsvej 47 ☎ 22 13 11 34, Ⓦ **restaurant-anarki.dk. Tues–Sat 5.30–10pm, Sun 5.30–11pm.**
Chef Rune Sauer Sonnichsen draws inspiration from all corners of the world and a multi-page global wine list attracts oenphiles to this bistro. The retro decor, such a vintage maps and low-lit green lamps, creates an intimate mood.

Bento

MAP P.80, POCKET MAP D8

Helgolandsgade 16 ☎ 88 71 46 46, Ⓦ **uki. dk. Tues–Sat 11am–2pm, 5–10pm.**
Family-run Japanese eatery with a traditional minimalist interior. Famous for its *makunouchi* (bento) boxes – from 298kr – it also excels in less pricey sushi and maki rolls, and has a well-stocked Japanese cocktail bar. Takeaway available.

Meyers Deli

Mother

Café Viggo

MAP P.80, POCKET MAP C8
Værnedamsvej 15 ☏ 33 31 18 21,
ⓦ cafeviggo.com. Mon–Wed 10am–
midnight, Thurs 10am–1am, Fri 10am–3am,
Sat 11am–3am.

Named after Belgian comic-book
character Gaston (Vakse Viggo
in Danish), this French-style
café-bistro is packed both day and
night. Apart from good, solid bistro
dishes such as quiche forestière
or steak haché, the chef excels in
genuine Breton *galettes*.

Cofoco

MAP P.80, POCKET MAP D8
Abel Cathrines Gade 7 ☏ 33 13 60 60,
ⓦ cofoco.dk. Daily 5.30pm–midnight.

Bright and modern, *Cofoco* sources
much of its food from the Baltic
island of Bornholm – where the
growing season is longer and
produce consequently tastier.
Dishes are superb but small
(75–85kr), the idea being that you
sample a range.

Famo

MAP P.80, POCKET MAP C8
Saxogade 3 ☏ 33 23 22 50, ⓦ famo.dk.

Daily 5.30pm–10pm.

Small, cheerful, no-frills Italian
restaurant serving a four-course
menu (350kr), prepared by a pair
of Michelin-starred chefs who have
decided to go it alone. Flavour-
packed delicacies might include
panzanella (Florentine bread-
and-tomato salad, crammed with
anchovies and herbs) and *ribolita*
(Tuscan bean soup).

Frk. Barners Kælder

MAP P.80, POCKET MAP D8
Helgolandsgade 8 ☏ 33 33 05 33,
ⓦ frkbarners.dk. Daily noon–4pm &
5.30–10pm.

With outdoor seating on a
streetside terrace and a cosy
cavern-like atmosphere inside, this
traditional restaurant – complete
with red-and-white-check
tablecloths – serves time-honoured
Danish classics such as herring
platters (98kr) at lunch, and
hakkebøf (Danish burger) with
potatoes, cucumber salad and fried
egg (159kr) at dinnertime.

Granola

MAP P.80, POCKET MAP C8

Værnedamsvej 5 ☎ 33 33 00 95, ⓦ granola.
dk. Mon–Wed 7.30am–11pm, Thurs & Fri
7.30am–midnight, Sat 9am–midnight, Sun
9am–5pm.

Retro-style milkshake bar whose
decor – including genuine
1930s ceiling lamps from the
Rover factory – shows staggering
attention to detail. Breakfast
(90–165kr, depending on size),
smoothies and juices are served
from early morning, while later on
the menu centres on well-prepared
home-made dishes such as quiches,
salads, sandwiches – and delicious
milkshakes, of course.

Hansens Gamle Familiehave

MAP P.80, POCKET MAP B8
Pile Alle 10 ☎ 36 30 92 57, ⓦ hansenshave.
dk. April–Sept 11am–midnight, rest of the
year Sun until 6pm.

In a pretty garden (with a
retractable winter roof) around
the corner from Frederiksberg
Slot this popular place excels in
smørrebrød (herring 59kr). There's
also a good range of traditional hot
dishes such as fried eel with parsley
sauce (239kr), and roast pork with
pickled red cabbage.

Kødbyens Fiskebar

MAP P.80, POCKET MAP D9
Flæsketorvet 100 ☎ 32 15 56 56,
ⓦ fiskebaren.dk. Daily 11.30am till late,
kitchen daily 11.30am–2.30pm & 6–11pm.

This super-trendy fish restaurant
in hip Kødbyen offers sustainably
sourced fresh fish and seafood, from
oysters (costing from 95kr for three)
to Norwegian scallop (165kr), the
menu varying according to the
season and catch. With whitewashed
walls and shiny black floors, it's also
a monument to cool industrial chic.

Lê Lê Nhà Hang

MAP P.80, POCKET MAP D8
Vesterbrogade 40 ☎ 53 73 73 73, ⓦ lele.
dk. Wed & Thurs 5–10pm, Fri & Sat
5–10.30pm.

This spacious Vietnamese place
serves gorgeous dishes which you

can watch being lovingly prepared
in the large open kitchen. Try for
instance the Saigonese papaya
salad with beef and Vietnamese
mint (85kr). Takeaway is available
further along the street at no. 56
(daily 10.30am–9.30pm).

Mad & Kaffe

MAP P.80, POCKET MAP C9
Sonder Blvd. 68 ☎ 31 35 08 80,
ⓦ madogkaffe.dk. Daily 8.30am–8pm.

With various locations across the
city, each café has its own stylish
and homey feel which resemble
the local areas. You can create
your own breakfast platters of
3, 5 or 7 items (94kr, 135kr or
165kr), with vegetarian and vegan
options. If you're not a brunch
person try the falafel burger
with home made fries (130kr).
Excellent coffee and cakes (40kr)
are available all day.

Madklubben Vesterbro

MAP P.80, POCKET MAP C8
Vesterbrogade 62 ☎ 38 41 41 43,
ⓦ madklubben.dk. Daily 5.30pm–midnight.

Simple, well-prepared dishes
in a funky, slightly space-age-
styled restaurant (part of a small
chain) right on the main drag of
Vesterbrogade. The straightforward
concept (choose from 1 to 3
courses, 124–225kr) is a big
hit with the Vesterbro crowd.
Favourite mains include the fish of
the day and the truffle-oil risotto
(both cost 100kr).

Mother

MAP P.80, POCKET MAP D8
Høkerboderne 9 ☎ 22 27 58 98, ⓦ mother.
dk. Daily 11am–1am.

Organic sourdough pizza served
in a long, rustic butcher's hall in
industrial-hip Kødbyen. *Mother*'s
chipper Italian proprietor, who
also mans the door, is kept busy
throughout the day as hungry diners
arrive in droves. Pizzas start at 75kr
for a filling Marinara. There is a small
but select wine list as well as full-
flavoured Menabrea beer on draught.

VESTERBRO AND FREDERIKSBERG

Paté Paté

MAP P.80, POCKET MAP D8

Slagterboderne 1 ☏ 39 69 55 57,
Ⓦ patepate.dk. Mon–Thurs 11.30am–10pm,
Fri 11.30amam–11pm, Sat noon–11pm,
Sun noon–10pm (April–Sept).

On-trend Kødbyen wine bar-cum-restaurant housed in a former meat pâté factory. Apart from a vast selection of great wines, *Paté Paté* also offers good, solid French food, with lighter bites on offer at lunchtime and dinner mains, which include grilled turbot (160kr) and beef tartare (125kr).

Riccos Kaffebar

MAP P.80, POCKET MAP C9

Istedgade 119 Ⓦ riccos.dk. Mon–Fri
8am–11pm, Sat & Sun 9am–11pm.

Riccos coffee shops have spread throughout the city but this is where it all started, and their unfaltering passion for good organic coffee is still in evidence. Packed into a tight space with only a few tiny tables and a long communal bench along the wall, coffee aficionados cram together here every morning for their caffeine fix.

Spuntino

MAP P.80, POCKET MAP C8

Vesterbrogade 68 ☏ 70 20 50 89, Ⓦ cofoco.
dk. Mon–Sun 5.30pm–midnight.

Part of the excellent Cofoco chain, no-frills *Spuntino* offers Italian classics such as *arancini*, braised lamb shank and *panna cotta*. Mix and match as you wish (65–100kr/dish) or go for the recommended seven-course menu (295kr).

Sticks'n'sushi

MAP P.80, POCKET MAP D9

Arni Magnussons Gade 2 ☏ 88 32 95 95,
Ⓦ sushi.dk. Sun–Wed 10am–11pm, Thurs &
Sat 10am–midnight.

Great-tasting sushi, seafood salads and Japanese dishes on the top floor of the twelve-storey *Tivoli Hotel*, with great views of Kødbyen and beyond.

Bars

Bang & Jensen

MAP P.80, POCKET MAP C8

Istedgade 130 ☏ 33 25 53 18,
Ⓦ bangogjensen.dk. Mon& Tues 7.30am–midnight, Wed–Fri 7.30am–2am, Sat
10am–2am, Sun 10am–midnight.

Housed in an old nineteenth-century chemist with high stucco ceilings, *Bang & Jensen* is a cosy neighbourhood café by day and a heaving bar at night. Saturday night features Ingeborg's Cocktail Salon, when you can enjoy a daiquiri or dry martini as the eponymous DJ spins some ambient tunes.

Curfew

MAP P.80, POCKET MAP D8

Stenosgade 1 ☏ 29 29 92 76, Ⓦ curfew.dk.
Tues–Thurs 6pm–2am, Fri 5pm–3am, Sat
6pm–3am.

Lavish cocktail bar inspired by the speakeasy culture of the 1920s and 1930s, run by flamboyant Portuguese-born cocktail aficionado, Humberto Marques. Also serves tapas.

Falernum

MAP P.80, POCKET MAP C8

Værnedamsvej 16 ☏ 33 22 30 89,
Ⓦ falernum.dk. Mon–Thurs noon–midnight,
Fri & Sat noon–2am, Sun noon–11am.

This snug wood-panelled wine bar offers most of its wines by the glass (from 60kr), with friendly and knowledgeable waiters on hand to share tasting notes. There's a wide range of food served throughout the day, such as home-made soup and an outstanding charcuterie platter.

Märkbar

MAP P.80, POCKET MAP C8

Vesterbrogade 106A ☏ 33 21 23 93. Tues–Wed 5pm–2am, Thurs–Sat 4pm–5am.

Dark, grungy, Berlin-inspired rock bar with a dependable crowd of regulars nodding their heads to the rhythm. A good range of beer, too.

Mesteren & Lærlingen

MAP P.80, POCKET MAP D9

Flæsketorvet 86 ☎ 32 15 24 83. Wed
8pm–1am, Thurs–Sat 8pm–3.30am.
Small, worn corner dive in Kødbyen
with a disc-juggling DJ on Friday
and Saturday. Music ranges from
Pink Floyd to African Soul.

Mikkeller

MAP P.80, POCKET MAP D8

Viktoriagade 8 ☎ 33 31 04 15, ⓦ mikkeller.
dk. Mon–Wed & Sun 1pm–1am, Thurs & Fri
1pm–2am, Sat noon–2am.
Mikkeller is a name whispered in
hushed reverential tones among
the beer cognoscenti, and this
intimate basement bar is a worthy
adjunct to the serious business of
brewing. A self-declared Carlsberg-
Free Zone, it offers a superb range
of innovative microbrewery ales,
including twenty on tap.

Salon 39

MAP P.80, POCKET MAP D7

Vodroffsvej 39 ☎ 31 39 11 39, ⓦ salon39.
dk. Wed–Sat from 3pm.
Frederiksberg's first cocktail bar,
this stylish, elegant place is now
also popular for the meals that

accompany the cocktails – such as,
the juicy 39 cheeseburger (149kr).

Vinbaren Vesterbro Torv

MAP P.80, POCKET MAP C8

Svendsgade 1 ☎ 21 40 85 27,
ⓦ vinbarenvesterbrotorv.dk. Mon–Thurs
3pm–midnight, Fri 3pm–2am.
Cosy, intimate wine bar with top
notch selection of wine from across
the world. Enjoy the occasional
live jazz music and the piano for
guests to play some tunes. If you've
enjoyed your wine from the bar,
you're in luck – the bottles are
available to take home.

Music venue

Vega

MAP P.80, POCKET MAP C9

Enghavevej 40 ☎ 33 25 70 11, ⓦ vega.dk.
One of the city's top live music
venues, housing three stages
with sublime sound featuring
well-established artists and bands
through the week. The attached
Ideal Bar offers a slightly lower-key
(and much smaller) venue for
catching up-and-coming local
bands (60–110kr) and DJs.

Mikkeller

Nørrebro and Østerbro

Beyond the city ramparts, the two neighbouring mid-nineteenth-century districts of Nørrebro and Østerbro are sometimes difficult to tell apart. This is despite deeply contrasting histories – Nørrebro's one of deprivation and social struggle followed by more recent immigration and gentrification, and Østerbro's characterized by traditional wealth and privilege. Aside from Copenhagen's most famous cemetery they lack standout tourist sights. They do, however, have plenty to offer when it comes to going out and having a good time with the locals. Squares such as trendy Sankt Hans Torv and multicultural Blågårds Plads in Nørrebro, and laidback Bopa Plads in Østerbro, are alive and kicking day and night, as is the once grimy Jægersborggade, now one of the city's most hyped streets, thanks mostly to the presence of a Michelin-starred restaurant.

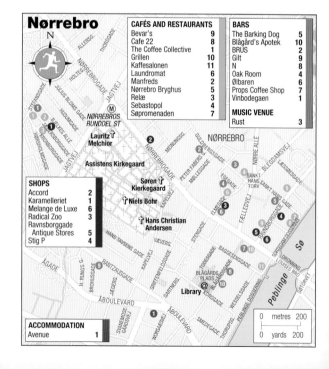

Nørrebro

N

CAFÉS AND RESTAURANTS	
Bevar's	9
Cafe 22	8
The Coffee Collective	1
Grillen	10
Kaffesalonen	11
Laundromat	6
Manfreds	2
Nørrebro Bryghus	5
Relæ	3
Sebastopol	4
Søpromenaden	7

BARS	
The Barking Dog	5
Blågård's Apotek	10
BRUS	2
Gilt	9
N	8
Oak Room	4
Ølbaren	6
Props Coffee Shop	7
Vinbodegaen	1

MUSIC VENUE	
Rust	3

SHOPS	
Accord	2
Karamelleriet	1
Melange de Luxe	6
Radical Zoo	3
Ravnsborggade Antique Stores	5
Stig P	4

ACCOMMODATION	
Avenue	1

Sankt Hans Torv

Assistens Kirkegaard

MAP P.88, POCKET MAP C5
Nørrebrogade April–Sept daily 7am–10pm,
Oct–March 7am–7pm. Entrances on
Nørrebrogade, Jagtvej and Kapelvej.
The tranquil leafy cemetery of
Assistens Kirkegaard was first
established in 1760 as a burial
place outside the city walls for its
poor and destitute. Since then,
and especially in the nineteenth
century during Copenhagen's
Golden Age of art and culture, it
became the city's most prestigious
and famous burial place. Most of
the graves are of the key movers
and shakers in the city's past.
Pick up one of the colourfully
dotted maps at one of the many
entrances, each colour representing
a profession, and you can make
your way around to find graves of
luminaries such as author Hans
Christian Andersen, philosopher
Søren Kirkegaard, Nobel-prize-
winning physicist Niels Bohr and
many, many more.

   While burials still occasionally
take place here, Assistens
Kirkegaard has more in common
with a regular park with its
wide tree-lined cycle paths
and picnickers and sunbathers
lounging about on warm days,
some using the tombstones as
back rests.

Fælledparken

MAP P.90, POCKET MAP E3–4
Fælledparken is at half a square
kilometre the city's largest park
used by over 11 million visitors
each year. It started life as a
common used to graze the city's
livestock. Later it became the
favoured haunt for the city's
gentlefolk on their Sunday
afternoon strolls. Today you'll
find all walks of life here, many
of them kicking a ball around
one of the six demarcated
football pitches. At the corner
near Trianglen a tranquil scent
garden has been designed for the
visually impaired, while across
Edel Sauntes Allé, you'll find the
4600-square-metre Fælledparken
Skatepark. On sunny days the

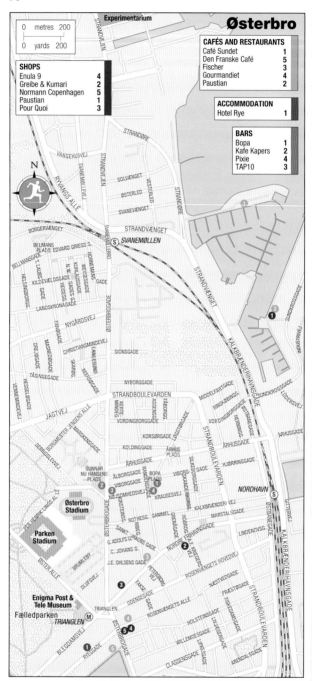

Østerbro

| 0 | metres | 200 |
| 0 | yards | 200 |

SHOPS
Enula 9	4
Greibe & Kumari	2
Normann Copenhagen	5
Paustian	1
Pour Quoi	3

CAFÉS AND RESTAURANTS
Café Sundet	1
Den Franske Café	5
Fischer	3
Gourmandiet	4
Paustian	2

ACCOMMODATION
| Hotel Rye | 1 |

BARS
Bopa	1
Kafe Kapers	2
Pixie	4
TAP10	3

Experimentarium

park becomes a patchwork of sunbathers' blankets and it's often difficult to find a spare patch of grass to settle on. Various events take place in Fælledparken throughout the year. Highlights include May Day and the annual carnival which both culminate here with lots of partying. In front of the park's small café there are also occasional gigs during summer, as well as weekly free Salsa lessons. Check out Ⓦ cafepavillonen.dk for details.

Enigma Post & Tele Museum

MAP P.90, POCKET MAP E4
Øster Allé 1 ☎ 33 41 09 00, Ⓦ enigma.dk. Daily 10am–4pm. Free.

After being closed down for replacement and modernization, the new museum is opening in phases, with the full museum in place by the end of 2020. The new *Enigma* name comes from the cipher machines that were used for commercial and military communication.

Enigma's facelift includes greater focus on the debates around current communications.

Experimentarium

MAP P.90, POCKET MAP F1
Tuborg Havnevej 7 ☎ 39 27 33 33, Ⓦ experimentarium.dk. Daily Mon–Thurs 9.30am–5pm, Fri–Sun 9.30am–7pm. 195kr over 11 years/115kr for 3–11 years.

Worth a detour if you have kids, **Experimentarium** is a giant hands-on science lab where you can test all sorts of things. The large permanent exhibit looks at the human body (avoid the section on sound waves if you don't like loud noises), how soap bubbles work, energy generation and much more. A large temporary exhibitions space often features blockbuster attractions on loan from other museums. Staff are at hand to show you what to do, if needed. Most children are worn out after a day of running around, pulling on ropes, pushing barrels, leaving parents free to do what they want afterwards.

NØRREBRO AND ØSTERBRO

Experimentarium

Shops

Accord

MAP P.88, POCKET MAP C5
Nørrebrogade 90 ☎ 70 15 16 17, ⓦ accord.
dk. Mon–Fri 10am–7pm, Sat 10am–5pm,
Sun noon–5pm.
This secondhand music store buys
and sells vinyl records, and is a
popular weekend hangout among
forty-something nostalgists, though
there's plenty here for younger
folk too.

Enula 9

MAP P.90, POCKET MAP F4
Rosenvængets Allé 6 ☎ 35 38 17 85,
ⓦ enula9.dk. Mon–Fri 11am–5.30pm, Sat
10am–3pm.
Tiny shop selling beautiful clothes
and accessories for pregnant
women and babies.

Greibe & Kumari

MAP P.90, POCKET MAP F3
Norde Frihavnsgade 60 ☎ 35 55 16 61.
Mon–Fri 11am–5.30pm, Sat 10am–2pm.
Luxury secondhand clothing
store where the richest and most
fashionable of Copenhagen society
drop off their designer cast-offs.
Barely worn examples of name
brands, including Scandinavian
labels Munthe and Filippa K.
Children's clothes too.

Karamelleriet

MAP P.88, POCKET MAP G4
Jægersborggade 36 ☎ 70 23 77 77, ⓦ kara
melleriet.com. Mon midday–5.30pm, Tues–Fri
10am–5.30pm, Sat & Sun 11am–3pm.
The sweet, smoky smell of burning
sugar lures innocent passersby into
this candy lair, where staff hand-pull
caramel before your eyes. Flavours
rane from salty liquorice to toffee.

Melange de Luxe

MAP P.88, POCKET MAP D6
Ravnsborggade 6 ☎ 22 63 65 75,
ⓦ melangedeluxe.dk. Mon–Fri 11am–6pm,
Sat 11am–5pm.
Small place selling secondhand
designer wear, including Gucci,

Prada and Chanel, at prices that
don't require a second mortgage.

Normann Copenhagen

MAP P.90, POCKET MAP F4
Østerbrogade 70 ☎ 35 55 44 59,
ⓦ normann-copenhagen.com. Mon–Fri
11am–5.30pm, Sat 10am–3pm.
A showcase for Nordic designer
homeware, with plenty of high-end
pieces as well as a few quirky and
affordable kitchen accessories. A
fun place to see what cutting-edge
creatives can think of next.

Paustian

MAP P.90, POCKET MAP G2
Kalkbrænderiløbskaj 2 ☎ 39 16 65 65,
ⓦ paustian.dk. Mon–Fri 11am–6pm, Sat &
Sun 10am–4pm.
Superb designer furniture sold in
a magnificent building designed
by Jørn Utzon of Sydney Opera
House fame. The vast range on
offer includes own-brand furniture
as well as iconic pieces such as
Alvar Aalto sofas and Verner
Panton chairs. There's also a stylish
restaurant (see page 95).

Pour Quoi

MAP P.90, POCKET MAP F4
Nordre Frihavnsgade 13 ☎ 35 26 62 54,
Mon–Fri 10am–6am, Sat 10am–2pm.
Cool clothes for women sold in
a compact three-storey shop with
heaps of fabulous dangly, glittering
accessories. Perfect for those lusting
after leopard-print leggings or a
unique T-shirt.

Radical Zoo

MAP P.88, POCKET MAP D5
Elmegade 19 ☎ 32 14 12 08. Mon–Thurs
11am–6pm, Fri & Sat 11am–7pm.
Small basement store selling
achingly on-trend clothes for men
and women from lesser known
Danish and international designers,
plus some own-brand creations.

Ravnsborggade Antique Stores

MAP P.88, POCKET MAP D6
The Nørrebrogade end of

Ravnsborggade is famous for its antique stores. Perusing these has become a popular Saturday morning treat and the prices have skyrocketed as a consequence. You may still be able to find some bargains if you dig around long enough.

Stig P

MAP P.88, POCKET MAP D5
Ravnsborggade 18 ☎ 70 22 86 18, ⓦ stigpofficial.com. Mon–Fri 11am–6pm, Sat 10am–4pm.
A minimalist, slimline shop selling quality ladieswear – own brand as well as international names such as Stella McCartney and Calvin Klein.

Cafés and restaurants

Bevar's

MAP P.88, POCKET MAP D5
Ravnsborggade 10B ☎ 50 59 09 93, ⓦ bevars.dk. Mon 9am–11pm, Tues & Wed 9am–midnight, Thurs 9am–2am, Fri & Sat until 3am, Sun 10am–10pm.
Relaxing retreat if you want to hide away and enjoy a good selection of drinks in a very comfortable armchair. A popular spot for students and workers, at night it transforms into a candlelit diner with live music.

Cafe 22

MAP P.88, POCKET MAP D5
Sortedams Dosseringen 21 ☎ 35 37 38 27, ⓦ cafe22.dk. Mon–Thurs 10am–11pm, Fri 10am–midnight, Sat 9am–midnight, Sun 9am–10pm.
Tucked away on a quiet corner, *Café 22* is a cosy basement café-restaurant with a string of popular lakeside tables with blankets available when the air gets chilly. Busy all day, from breakfast onwards; the good-value menu includes a mouthwatering veggie or meaty brunch (85kr).

Café Sundet

MAP P.90, POCKET MAP F1
Svaneknoppen 2, Svanemøllen ☎ 39 29 30

Fischer

35, ⓦ cafesundet.dk. Daily 11am–10pm.
On the first floor of the Svanemøllen sailing clubhouse with wonderful views of Øresund, *Café Sundet* is the perfect place for a leisurely lunch. The focus is naturally on seafood – such as grilled salmon with saffron sauce (179kr) – but you also won't go wrong either with their salads or "light" lasagna (from 50kr).

Den Franske Café

MAP P.90, POCKET MAP E4
Sortedams Dosseringen 101 ☎ 35 42 48 45, ⓦ denfranskecafe.dk. Mon–Fri 8am–11pm, Sat & Sun 9am–11pm.
At the posh Østerbro end of the lake, this delightful café with outdoor seating on the lakeside promenade features French-style decor and a few Gallic touches on the menu – freshly baked croissants for example. You'll also find classic Danish rye-bread sandwiches plus some very tasty burgers (around 120kr) served with home-made *frites*.

Fischer

MAP P.90, POCKET MAP F4
Victor Borges Plads 12 ☎ 35 42 39 64,

Ⓦ hosfischer.dk. Mon–Sun 5–10.30pm.
Compact and romantic little
Italian trattoria in the heart
of Østerbro, just off Nordre
Frihavnsgade, offering flavour-
packed Roman dishes – such as
guancia di maiale con fagioli (pork
cheeks stuffed with cowberries)
– a result of the chef's many
years of training in Rome. Primi
pasta dishes from 125kr; secondi
around 235kr.

Gourmandiet

MAP P.90, POCKET MAP F4
Rosenvænget Allé 7A Ⓣ 39 27 10 00,
Ⓦ gourmandiet.dk. Tues–Thurs 11am–6pm,
Fri 11am–7pm, Sat 10am–3pm.
Gourmandiet is a traditional
butcher's shop – evident in the
beautiful old tiling – which
has evolved into an excellent
charcuterie-cum-restaurant.
Although open for brunch on
Saturdays, and with a lunchtime
menu comprising an extensive
selection of delicious cold cuts
during the week, it's the juicy
organic steak three nights a week
that's the star attraction.

Manfreds

Grillen

MAP P.88, POCKET MAP D6
Nørrebrogade 12 Ⓣ 35 35 35 69,
Ⓦ grillenburgerbar.dk. Sun–Wed 11.30am–
10pm, Thurs–Sat 11.30am–11pm.
If you are in need for a juicy burger
with a good portion of fries, this is
the place to go. You can create your
own burger (from 89k) or choose
one of the 8 different burgers from
the menu and add one of the 5
different kinds of fries and mayo.

Kaffesalonen

MAP P.88, POCKET MAP D6
Peblinge Dosseringen 6 Ⓣ 35 35 12 19,
Ⓦ kaffesalonen.com. Mon–Fri 8am–
midnight, Sat & Sun 10am–midnight.
An old lakeside favourite which
started life as a breakfast/coffee
shop for workers on their way
home from the nightshift and now
offers delicious meals throughout
the day, including grilled goat's
cheese salad and ribeye steak served
with all the trimmings. Weather
permitting, service extends to a
lakeside pontoon with a lively bar
– especially worth dropping by on
Midsummer's Eve.

Laundromat

MAP P.88, POCKET MAP D5
Elmegade 15 Ⓣ 35 35 26 72,
Ⓦ thelaundromatcafe.com. Daily
9am–9pm.
Hugely successful Icelandic concept
café which combines laundromat,
library and café in one, around
the corner from trendy Sankt
Hans Torv. Their weekend brunch
(145kr) comes recommended,
having won several awards, but the
place is busy all day with students
sipping coffee and people making
use of the free wi-fi.

Manfreds

MAP P.88, POCKET MAP C5
Jægersborggade 40 Ⓣ 36 96 65 93,
Ⓦ manfreds.dk. Daily noon–3.30pm &
5–10pm.
New Nordic fine dining in an
informal, intimate setting. The
food is adventurous featuring

ingredients such as duck gizzard and unripe peaches, prepared to perfection in a sharing menu that will set you back 250kr per person. There's also a good-value French-style weekday lunch (five courses for 195kr) and a unique wine list featuring "biodynamic" wines.

Nørrebro Bryghus

MAP P.88, POCKET MAP D5
Ryesgade 3 ☎ 35 30 05 30,
ⓦ noerrebrobryghus.dk. Mon–Thurs noon–11pm, Fri & Sat noon–1am.
Microbrewery-cum-restaurant where you can try beer-glazed cauliflower and *panna cotta* served with beer syrup. Surprisingly, it all does seem to work, and the long wood-beamed tables are packed to capacity most nights. Hour-long brewery tours led by the chief brewer (145kr) include four samples en route.

Paustian

MAP P.90, POCKET MAP G2
Kalkbrænderiløbskaj 2 ☎ 39 18 55 01,
ⓦ restaurantpaustian.dk. Mon–Sat 10.30am–3.30pm.
Buzzy restaurant attached to the top-of-the-range designer furniture store (see p.100). The lunchtime menu of herring, smørrebrød and salads (from 95kr) provides a delicious break from furniture perusing.

Relæ

MAP P.88, POCKET MAP C5
Jægersborggade 41 ☎ 36 96 66 09,
ⓦ restaurant-relae.dk. Tues–Sat 5–midnight, lunch Fri & Sat noon–3pm.
Probably the only Michelin-starred restaurant in Copenhagen that won't break the bank (the four-course tasting menu costs 495kr). Expect unusual Nordic fusion food such as carrots, elderflower and sesame. The emphasis is on the dining experience and you may end up squeezed a little tight in this unpretentious basement restaurant. Reserve a table well in advance – there are also a few counter settings facing the kitchen available at short notice.

Sebastopol

MAP P.88, POCKET MAP D5
Sankt Hans Torv 32 ☎ 35 36 30 02,
ⓦ sebastopol.dk. Mon–Thurs & Sun 10am–9.30pm, Fri & Sat 10am–10.30am.
A Copenhagen fixture since 1994, *Sebastopol* offers a touch of Parisian café chic on trendy Sankt Hans Torv. It's often packed with arty Nørrebro types indulging in a leisurely brunch (from 90kr). Later in the day the French bistro menu includes dishes such as steak tartare or *moules frites* (180kr). With south-facing seating outside on the square, *Sebastopol* is also a popular place for a sundowner drink.

Søpromenaden

MAP P.88, POCKET MAP D5
Sortedam Dosseringen 103 ☎ 35 42 66 06,
ⓦ søpromenaden.dk. Daily 11am–10.30pm.
With checked tablecloths and a lovely lakeside setting, *Søpromenaden* emanates rural charm even though it's at the lake's busy and chic Østerbro end. Menu highlights include an extensive lunchtime smørrebrød list and all-time Danish classics such as *frikadeller* and *rødkål* – meatballs served with pickled red cabbage (159kr).

Bars

The Barking Dog

MAP P.88, POCKET MAP D5
Sankt Hans Gade 19 ☎ 35 36 16 00,
ⓦ thebarkingdog.dk. Mon & Sun 4pm–midnight, Tues–Thurs 4pm–1am, Fri & Sat 4pm–2am.
When you've had enough of the city's uber-stylish offerings this relaxed neighbourhood pub may come in handy. Featuring a small selection of beers (including a few from Nørrebros Bryghus) and wine, *The Barking Dog* also makes a mean Power's Sour cocktail; ask the waiter for the story.

Blågård's Apotek

MAP P.88, POCKET MAP D6
Blågårds Plads 2 ☎ 35 37 24 42. Mon–Sat

noon–2am, Sun noon–10pm.

Known as *Kroteket* ('The Barmacy') to locals, this café – turns bar at night – used to be an old pharmacy. If you look closely you can still see some old pharmacy details like the old pharmacist's desk. This non-profit café hosts many social events and showcases local arts but besides that it's best known for the wide selection of beers, amazing atmosphere and knowledgeable staff.

Bopa

MAP P.90, POCKET MAP F3
Løgstørgade 8 ☎ 35 43 05 66, Ⓦ cafebopa.
dk. Mon–Thurs 9am–midnight, Fri
9am–3am, Sat 10am–3am, Sun 10am–
midnight.
Cosy café-bar which gets packed most weekends after 11.30pm when a DJ hits the turntables. Excellent range of beers including some from the Skovlyst Brewery north of the city which uses quirky ingredients such as nettles and beech syrup.

BRUS

MAP P.88, POCKET MAP D5
Guldbergsgade 29 ☎ 75 22 22 00,
Ⓦ tapperietbrus.dk. Mon–Thurs 3pm–
midnight, Fri midday–3am, Sat 11am–3am,
Sun 11am–midnight.
Launched by students of Copenhagen's top craft brewer *Mikkeller*, BRUS combines a brewery with a good-looking minimalist bar, a shop and restaurant. There are 20 roating beers on tap, all from microbrewery To Øl.

Gilt

MAP P.88, POCKET MAP C6
Rantzausgade 39 ☎ 27 26 80 70, Ⓦ gilt.dk.
Wed–Sat 6pm–late.
"Honest and unadulterated classic cocktails" goes the sales pitch at this stylish little bar. While you might persuade them to knock up a martini, the emphasis here is on Nordic-inspired concoctions using unusual ingredients such

as dandelion syrup and roasted pine needles.

Kafe Kapers

MAP P.90, POCKET MAP E3
Gunnar Nu Hansens Plads 2 ☎ 35 25 11 20,
Ⓦ kafekapers.dk. Daily 9am–midnight.
On a square a short walk from Fælledparken (see page 89), *Kapers* is basically a glass cube encased in a large marquee. The outdoor seating area is a popular place to watch the world go by throughout the year (heaters and blankets provided in winter).

N

MAP P.88, POCKET MAP D6
Blågårdsgade 17 ☎ 32 15 68 52,
Ⓦ cafe-n-2200.dk. Daily 8.30am–11pm.
A chilled-out little place with long tables and benches on lively Blågårdsgade and the perfect spot to absorb the day's last rays of sunshine. Drinks on offer include organic beer and wine, and some wonderful fresh juices.

Oak Room

MAP P.88, POCKET MAP D5
Birkegade 10 ☎ 38 60 38 60, Ⓦ oakroom.
dk. Tues & Wed 6pm–1am, Thurs 7pm–2am,
Fri & Sat 6pm–4am.
Super-cool, Mad-Men-esque cocktail bar whose sleek interior, designed by cutting-edge architect Kasper Røøn, transports you back to those heady 1960s days of Danish Functionalism. Don't miss the Venezuelan Butterfly (made with passion fruit, mint and rum), the all-time classic.

Ølbaren

MAP P.88, POCKET MAP D5
Elmegade 2 ☎ 35 35 45 34, Ⓦ oelbaren.dk.
Mon–Wed 6pm–1am, Thurs 4pm–2am, Fri
& Sat 2pm–2am, Sun 2–11pm.
A small, bar run for and by beer nerds – and proud of it. Don't expect conversation to drift far from the favoured subject – brews from around the globe – and you'll be fine. Featuring over one hundred different labels, there's plenty to talk about.

Pixie

MAP P.90, POCKET MAP F3

Løgstørgade 2 ☎ 39 30 03 05, ⓦ cafepixie.
dk. Mon–Thurs 8am–midnight, Fri 8.30am–
3am, Sat 10am–3am, Sun 10am–10pm.
Facing a small playground on
Bopa Plads, *Pixie* is an authentic
neighbourhood café (breakfasts
from 50kr), popular with
parents relaxing on the outdoor
terrace. Occasional live music in
the evenings.

Props Coffee Shop

MAP P.88, POCKET MAP D6

Blågårdsgade 5 ☎ 35 36 99 55,
ⓦ propscoffeeshop.dk.
Quirky bar-cum-café with a slightly
chaotic, laidback atmosphere.
All of its rickety furniture is
for sale – look out for the price
tag underneath.

TAP10

MAP P.90, POCKET MAP E3

Østerbrogade 122 ☎ 61 72 44 87. Tues
4pm–midnight, Wed 3pm–midnight, Thurs
4pm–1am, Fri & Sat 2pm–2am.
At the top end of Østerbrogade
close to Bopa Plads, this trendy
basement bar specializes in Nordic
craft beers, with more Scandi-brews

chalked up on the board than
you could imagine, many of them
on draught.

Vinbodegaen

MAP P.88, POCKET MAP C5

Jægersborggade 56 ☎ 38 11 30 30,
ⓦ vinbodegaen.dk. Tues & Wed 5–11pm,
Thurs 5pm–midnight, Fri 2pm–1am, Sat
1pm–1am.
Located on uber-trendy foodie
street Jægersborggade and owned
by the man behind *Bibendum* (see
page 68), the cure offered by
Vinbodegaen wine bar is in the form
of choice wines from Husted Vin
and delicious comfort food, served
outside in summer.

Music venue

Rust

MAP P.88, POCKET MAP D5

Guldbergsgade 8 ☎ 35 24 52 00, ⓦ rust.dk.
Wed–Sat 9pm–5am.
Three floors of live music with
edgy, experimental as well as more
mainstream acts and a kickass
clubbing scene too (40–60kr).
Named after Cold War aviator
Mathias Rust.

Ølbaren

Day-trips

An afternoon away from the big city is essential for getting to know a gentler, quieter Denmark. Copenhagen is just a short train ride or even cycle from some stellar destinations in greater Zealand. If you're staying in town for more than just a day or two, you'll definitely want to venture north on a train (and take your rented cycle with you if you like) for art museums, parklands and castles galore – including the very fortress that inspired Shakespeare's Elsinore Castle in *Hamlet*. South, meanwhile, you'll find beaches, quiet townships, more art and Scandinavia's biggest and best aquarium.

Dyrehaven and Bakken

MAP P.100
Klampenborg S-Tog station. Bakken ☎ 39 63 35 44, ⓦ bakken.dk. End of March to end of Aug daily 9am–5pm & 9am–4.30pm. Admission free; multi-ride pass 249kr, children 179kr.

A short walk from Klampenborg S-Tog station, the largely forested **Dyrehaven** (Deer Park) was established in 1669 as a royal hunting ground, and is still home to some two thousand (fairly

Dyrehaven

tame) red, sika and fallow deer. It's a picturesque spot, with the ancient oak and beech woodland an atmospheric backdrop, particularly in the early morning mist. Poised on a hilltop in the middle of the park is the **Eremitageslotten** (Ermitage Palace), a grand hunting lodge built for Christian VI in 1736, though it's closed to the public.

Occupying part of the park's southern section, **Bakken** is supposedly the oldest still-functioning amusement park in the world, tracing its origins back to 1583 when entertainers first set up business next to Kirsten Piil's holy spring. It lacks the polish or refinement of Tivoli – but with 33 rides and almost as many places to drink, there's plenty of fun to be had, not least at weekends when the place can be heaving.

Louisiana

MAP P.100
Humlebæk train station, from which it's a 10min walk (follow the signs) ☎ 49 19 07 19, ⓦ louisiana.dk. Tues–Fri 11am–10pm, Sat & Sun 11am–6pm. 115kr.

A perfect fusion of art, architecture and landscape, **Louisiana Museum of Modern Art** – with good reason Denmark's most visited art gallery – has a setting nearly as magical as the museum itself. Overlooking

Rocking Roskilde

The carnivalesque **Roskilde festival** (ⓦroskilde-festival.com) might be Europe's single best open-air event, commonly drawing some 100,000 people. At the end of June, throngs of Danish teens, kidults and ageing hipsters descend on a Roskilde farm to hear more than 150 Scandinavian and international acts take to the eight stages. Pharrell Williams and Paul McCartney were recent performers, but Roskilde is best for lesser-known acts. Logistically it's surprisingly efficient, with free camping next to the festival site and shuttle buses from the train station. Tickets are priced around 2000kr and regularly sell out, so plan in advance.

Roskilde (30min by train from Copenhagen) was thus the obvious location for **Denmark's Rock Museum**, which opened in the vibrant Musicon district at the end of 2015. Also worth a look is the **Viking Ship Museum** (daily 10am–4pm/5pm in summer; 110/150kr; ⓦvikingeskibsmuseet.dk), home to five well-preserved Viking longships. In summer you can row a modern version in the harbour.

the Øresund strait, the museum began life in 1958, when a series of interconnecting glass pavilions was built around a nineteenth-century villa, Louisiana (named after the original owner's three wives, each of whom, oddly enough, was called Louise) – the ensemble landscaped within an outdoor sculpture park. Louisiana's collection grew quickly and the museum is now home to over three thousand permanent works from around the globe, many world-class.

The entrance is in the main villa, from which – moving clockwise into the west wing – you first reach a light, open space primarily used for temporary shows; exhibitions in recent years have included Andy Warhol, David Hockney, Ai Weiwei and Emil Nolde. Next, housed in a purpose-built gallery, is an outstanding collection of **Giacometti**'s gaunt sculptures and drawings, which leads on to the museum's extensive and colourful collection of abstract works by **CoBrA** (see page 62). Major Danish artists such as Henrik Heerup and Asger Jorn – who has a special room dedicated to his art – are featured alongside.

From the museum café, with its outdoor terrace overlooking Øresund, a subterranean section of graphic art leads onto another of the museum's highlights, the permanent exhibition in the museum's south wing, which focuses on **Constructivism** with works by the likes of Vasarely, Albers and Soto. **Nouveau Réalisme** is represented with pieces by Yves Klein, César and Raysse among others, while Lichtenstein, Rauschenberg, Warhol and Oldenburg lead the charge for the **Pop Art** and **Minimalism** collections.

Outside, on the lawns sloping down towards the coast, the **sculpture garden** is home to around sixty works including Max Ernst, Henri Laurens, Miró and Henry Moore.

Frederiksborg Slot

MAP P.100
S-Tog line E to Hillerød, then bus #301 to Ullerød or #302 to Sophienlund ⓣ48 26 04 39, ⓦdnm.dk. Daily April–Oct 10am–5pm; Nov–March 11am–3pm. 75kr.

Glorious **Frederiksborg Slot** lies decorously across three small islands within an artificial lake, and

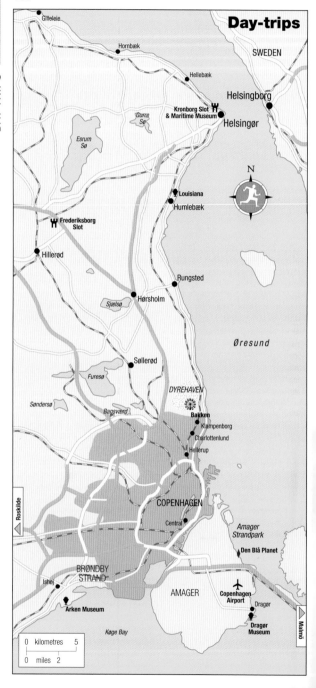

Day-trips

Gilleleje

Hornbæk

Hellebæk

SWEDEN

Helsingborg

Kronborg Slot
& Maritime Museum

Helsingør

Gurre Sø

Esrum Sø

N

Louisiana

Humlebæk

Frederiksborg Slot

Hillerød

Rungsted

Sjælsø

Hørsholm

Øresund

Søllerød

Furesø

Søndersø

DYREHAVEN

Bagsværd

Bakken

Klampenborg

Charlottenlund

Hellerup

Roskilde

COPENHAGEN

Central

Amager Strandpark

Den Blå Planet

BRØNDBY STRAND

Ishøj

AMAGER

Copenhagen Airport

Dragør

Malmö

Arken Museum

Dragør Museum

Køge Bay

| 0 | kilometres | 5 |
| 0 | miles | 2 |

is set within magnificent Baroque gardens. It was originally the home of Frederik II and birthplace of his son Christian IV, who, at the beginning of the seventeenth century, had it rebuilt in an unorthodox Dutch Renaissance style. It's the unusual aspects of the design – a prolific use of towers and spires, Gothic arches and flowery window ornamentation – that still stand out.

Since 1882, the interior has functioned as a **Museum of National History** with sixty-odd rooms charting Danish history since 1500. Many are surprisingly free of furniture and household objects, drawing attention instead to the ranks of portraits along the walls – a motley crew of flat-faced kings and thin consorts who between them ruled and misruled Denmark for centuries.

Kronborg Slot

MAP P.100
Helsingør train station, from which it's a 15min walk ☎ 49 21 30 78, ⓦ kronborg.dk. Easter–May & Sept & Oct daily 11am–4pm; June–Aug daily 10am–5.30pm; Nov–Easter Tues–Sun 11am–4pm. Jan–May & Sept–

Dec 95kr, Jun–Aug 145kr. Guided tours of the royal chambers in English daily at 11.30am and 1.30pm; of the casemates daily 12.30pm.

Tactically placed on a sandy curl of land extending seawards into the Øresund some 45km north of Copenhagen in the city of Helsingør, **Kronborg Slot** is impossible to miss. It's known primarily – under the name of Elsinore Castle – as the setting for Shakespeare's *Hamlet*, though it's uncertain whether the playwright actually ever visited Helsingør.

Constructed in the fifteenth century by Erik of Pomerania, the original fortress of Krogen was for hundreds of years the key to control of the Øresund (Helsingborg on the other side of the strait was also under Danish rule), enabling the Danish monarchs to extract a toll from every ship that passed through it.

Maritime Museum of Denmark

MAP P.100
Kronborg Slot ☎ 49 21 06 85, ⓦ mfs.dk. July & Aug daily 10am–6pm; Sept–June Tues–Sun 11am–5pm. 120kr.

Maritime Museum of Denmark

Den Blå Planet

This museum is set underground in the old dry docks next to Kronborg Castle. The structure comprises a continuous ramp looping around the dock walls, allowing for unobstructed views of the castle. Inside, informative and interactive exhibits span Viking, medieval and modern seafaring, exploration and merchant shipping (including a colossal Maersk freight container).

Amager Strandpark

MAP P.100
Metro to Øresund Station or bus #77 or #78.

Just to the southeast of the centre of Copenhagen, beyond Christianshavn, is the large island of **Amager**. On its east coast, with fine views of the Øresunds Bridge, **Amager Strandpark** is one of the city's most popular summer getaways, with around 5km of beautiful, soft sandy beaches. The beautifully restored traditional wooden **Helgoland Søbadeanstalt**, where Øresundsvej meets Amager Strandvej, offers free changing facilities and showers (late June to end of Aug; free); while at the southern end, **Kastrup Søbad** (June Mon–Fri 3–6pm, July to

mid-Sept Mon–Fri 11am–8pm, Sat & Sun 11am–8pm; free) has a 5m-high trampoline which provides a fabulous launch pad into the water.

Connected to "mainland" Amager by three short bridges is an artificial island some 2km long, with a shallow lagoon, popular for kitesurfing, windsurfing and kayaking and ideal for kids to paddle in. There are toilets and showers all along the beach, and at its southern end a couple of good places to eat (see page 104).

Den Blå Planet

MAP P.100
Metro to Kastrup Station, from which it's a 10min walk ⓘ 44 22 22 44, ⓦ denblaaplanet.dk. Mon 10am–9pm, Tues–Sun 10am–5pm. 170kr, children 3–11yrs 95kr.

In a spectacular waterside position next to Kastrup marina, **Den Blå Planet** (The Blue Planet) is the state-of-the-art home for Denmark's National Aquarium – the largest in Northern Europe. All curves, it's a remarkable structure, shaped – when viewed from the air – like a giant whirlpool, with five "arms" radiating from the vortex centre, a circular foyer. Each arm represents a different environment: habitats range from a sunken Amazon forest, featuring Europe's largest school of piranhas, to a Faroese bird cliff, complete with puffins and divers. Highlight for many, though, is undoubtedly the walk through the huge "ocean" aquarium tunnel, with hammerhead sharks and manta rays swimming above and below you and inquisitive sea lions pressing up to the glass. The building has already won several design awards, and is among the best spots in the city to cut loose (and curry favour with) the kids for an afternoon.

Arken Museum of Modern Art

MAP P.100

Train to Ishøj station, then bus #128 (10min), or a 20min walk ☎ 43 54 02 22, ⓦ arken.dk. Tues & Thurs–Sun 10am–5pm, Wed 10am–9pm. 125kr.

Smaller and more manageable than Louisiana or the Statens Museum for Kunst, the **Arken Museum for Moderne Kunst** (Arken Museum of Modern Art), just outside the coastal town of Ishøj about 20km southwest of Copenhagen, is well worth seeking out both for its architecture and for its content. Paying homage to its bleak position in front of a windswept sandy beach, architect Søren Robert Lund designed the museum to resemble a shipwreck, its prow thrusting dramatically up from among the dunes. The museum is known for its excellent temporary exhibitions – recent shows have covered eco architect Hundertwasser and Danish artist of the 1920s and 1930s, Gerda Wegener– though these merely supplement a permanent display that focuses on contemporary art from the 1990s onwards and includes pieces by Damien Hirst, Antony Gormley, Jeff Koons and Grayson Perry as well as Danish artists Per Kirkeby and Asger Jorn. Its café is also well worth a visit (see page 104).

Dragør

MAP P.100

Tårnby Station, then bus #350S to the end. Museum: ☎ 30 10 88 68, ⓦ museumamager.dk. May & Sept Sat & Sun noon–4pm; June & end Aug Thurs–Sun noon–4pm; July to mid-Aug Tues–Sun noon–4pm. 40kr, children free.

South of Copenhagen Airport, in the southeasternmost corner of Amager, lies the atmospheric cobblestoned fishing village of **Dragør**, formerly the departure point for ferries to Sweden. It now mainly survives on tourism and the high incomes of its city-commuting inhabitants – properties in Dragør do not come cheap. Apart from meandering around the quaint streets, and lazing on the peaceful south coast beaches, while here you could check out the **Dragør Museum**, devoted to the maritime history of the village from the thirteenth-century herring trade to the arrival of the Dutch in the early sixteenth century. At the time of writing the museum was closed and due to open with updated exhibits in 2020.

Arken Museum of Modern Art

Cafés and restaurants

Arken Café

Skovvej 100, Ishøj ☎ 51 67 02 23, 🌐 arken.
dk. Tues & Thurs–Sun 10am–4.30pm, Wed
10am–8.30pm.

Beautiful salmon platters (139kr)
and sandwiches served in an elegant
café upstairs in the museum, with
sweeping views of marram-grass-
covered dunes and the deep blue
sea in the distance. The menu
also includes a handful of tasty
hot dishes – baked cod with kale,
for instance –and the obligatorily
excellent cake (35kr).

Café Baaden

Havkajakvej 16, Amager Strandpark ☎ 28
72 73 02, 🌐 cafebaaden.dk. Mon–Fri
11am–8pm, Sat & Sun from 10am.

A modern houseboat in a fine
setting on Amager Strandpark,
making it Denmark's only café
on the water. They serve anything
from scrumptious brunch platters
(139kr), spicy burgers (145kr)
to quinoa tabbouleh (125kr). Or
enjoy a nice glass of champagne
while looking out over the sea, you
may even see Sweden.

Arken Café

Café Kystens Perle

Bryggergården 14, Kastrup ☎ 32 50 40
19, 🌐 cafekystensperle.dk. Mon–Fri
11am–10pm, Sat & Sun 10am–10pm.

A short walk from Den Blå Planet,
this striking eighteenth-century
restaurant was once a brewery.
With its crooked walls and low
ceilings the "Pearl of the Coast" has
retained some of its old-fashioned
ambience while its front terrace
provides great coastal views. Food
is served throughout the day,
including brunch (fruit platter
45kr), a lunchtime smørrebrød
platter (159kr) and burgers (155kr)
and steak later in the day.

Café Sylten

Søndre Strandvej 50, Dragør ☎ 30 50 60 19,
🌐 sylten.dk. Mon–Fri noon–11pm, Sat &
Sun 11am–11pm.

Hidden away among the dunes a
stone's throw from the beach just
south of Dragør, this old dark-
wood cabin is a wonderful place
to catch the sunset on a summer
evening. Come for a drink on the
terrace (there's a small but select
beer and wine list) or to sample
some hearty meat dishes (from
150kr). At weekends there's a
brunch buffet (179kr; 11am–2pm).

Dragør Røgeri

Gammel Havn 6–8, Dragør ☎ 32 53 06 03,
🌐 dragor-rogeri.dk. Sept Wed–Sun 10am–
5pm, Oct–Dec Thurs–Sun 10am–5pm.

Authentic smokehouse at Dragør
harbour that sells an enormous
array of freshly caught and freshly
smoked seafood, including
legendary smoked eel and herring.
They're suppliers to the main
restaurants in the city but you can
cut out the middleman and enjoy
their home-made *fiskefrikadeller og
remoulade* (fishcakes with tartare
sauce) or fried plaice and chips
(both 65kr) at their harbourfront
picnic table for half the price.

Peter Lieps Hus

Dyrehaven 8 ☎ 39 64 07 86, 🌐 peterliep.
dk. Tues–Sun 11am–5pm.

Café Kystens Perle

Quaint thatched restaurant on a busy pedestrian junction at the edge of Dyrehaven woods, not far from the Bakken amusement park. Lunch at *Peter Lieps* is a popular weekend treat for busy city folk, with a menu focusing primarily on smørrebrød – with an extensive list of over twenty toppings – and classics such as a delicious venison burger made with local game. Mains are in the 150–250kr range.

Restaurant Piil & Co

Dyrehaven 7, Klampenborg ☏ 70 26 02 12, Ⓦ piil-co.dk. Daily noon–6pm.
Tucked away in Dyrehaven next to the famous holy spring of Kirsten Piil and overlooking a lake, this romantic log cabin is a great place for pancakes and hot chocolate after a day in the woods. For more substantial dining there is also an excellent lunchtime spread of smørrebrød classics and a few à la carte dishes such as saddle of pork with apple and crackling (125kr). Just a ten-minute walk from Klampenborg station.

Spisestedet Leonora

Frederiksborg Slot, Møntportevej 2, Hillerød ☏ 48 26 75 16, Ⓦ leonora.dk. Daily: 10am–5pm
Housed in one of Frederiksborg Slot's former stables, with seating outside in the palace courtyard in summertime, *Leonora* serves a traditional Danish lunch that's fit for a king. Lavishly presented smørrebrød, tartlets overflowing with asparagus and chicken, fillets of plaice served with prawns and caviar, all very reasonably priced.

Bar

Sukaiba

AC Hotel Bella Sky, Ørestaden. Take metro to Bella Center or bus #30 from Vesterport ☏ 88 77 97 97, Ⓦ sukaiba. dk. Mon–Wed 5.30pm–midnight, Thurs & Fri 5.30pm–1am, Sat 11am–1am, Sun 11am–3am.
On the top floor of the extraordinary *AC Hotel Bella Sky* – a vast, 814-room complex – Japanese fushion restaurant and bar *Sukaiba* provides breathtaking views of the city skyline, all the way to Sweden. It's accessed via the super-cool aerial walkway that links the two twisting leaning towers. Splash out on the sixteen-course tasting menu for 895kr. Drinks are worth sampling, too: there's a good selection of cocktails; try the Sadayakko a shiitake mushroom-infused Japanese whisky concoction (130kr).

Malmö

Just a short hop across the water from Copenhagen, the Swedish city of Malmö makes for a tempting day-trip. Once part of Denmark (the Danes spell it "Malmø"), it was acquired by the Swedish king Karl X in 1658 along with Skåne (Scania), the surrounding province. Today Malmö is Sweden's third largest city, an attractive mix of chocolate-box medieval squares and striking modern architecture, most notably the Turning Torso skyscraper, Scandinavia's tallest building. You'll also find it a cosmopolitan, culturally diverse population – more than a hundred languages are spoken on its streets and Turkish and Thai food are as popular as meatballs and herring.

Stortorget and Lilla Torg

The city's main square, **Stortorget** is as impressive today as it must have been when it was first laid out in the sixteenth century. It's flanked on one side by the imposing **Rådhus**, built in 1546 and covered with statuary and spiky accoutrements. To its rear stands the fine Gothic **St Petri Kyrka** (daily 10am–6pm; free) while to the south runs **Södergatan**, Malmö's main pedestrianized shopping street.

Turning Torso

A late sixteenth-century spin-off from Stortorget, **Lilla Torg** is everyone's favourite part of the city. Lined with cafés and restaurants, it's usually pretty crowded at night, with drinkers kept warm under patio heaters and bars handing out free blankets.

Malmöhus Castle

MAP P.107,
Malmöhusvägen ☏ 040 34 44 00,
🅦 malmo.se. Daily 10am–5pm. 40SEK.
The princely **Malmöhus** is a low fortified castle defended by a wide moat and two circular keeps. Built by Danish king Christian III in 1536, the castle was later used for a time as a prison, but it now houses the **Malmö Museer**, a disparate but fascinating collection of exhibitions on everything from geology to photography – and an aquarium, too. The pleasant grounds, the **Kungsparken**, are peppered with small lakes and an old windmill.

Moderna Muséet

MAP P.107,
Ola Billgrens plats 2–4 ☏ 046 852 02
3500, 🅦 modernamuseet.se. Tues–Sun
11am–6pm. Free.
This branch of Stockholm's famous modern art museum hosts excellent

Visiting Malmö

Frequent **trains** (34min; 90kr) connect Copenhagen with Malmö, across the 16km Öresund Bridge/tunnel link. You arrive in the bowels of Malmö's rebuilt Central Station. **Malmö Airport** is located 30km to the east with frequent bus connections into the city as well as to Copenhagen. The **tourist office**, opposite the train station at Skeppsbron 2 (Mon–Fri 9am–5pm, Sat & Sun 9am–2pm, reduced hours in winter ☎ 040 34 12 00, ⓦ malmotown.com), sells the Malmö City Card (100SEK), a voucher book (also available as an app) offering a range of discounts. Many shops accept Danish kroner though at an uncompetitive 1–1 rate so it's usually best to convert to Swedish currency (SEK).

temporary exhibitions. The building itself is worth a visit for the striking orange-red cube extension built on to what was the city's electricity works.

The Turning Torso

A good twenty-minute walk or five-minute cycle ride north of the station is Malmö's most iconic sight, the 190m **Turning Torso** skyscraper. A spiralling helix of glass and steel, the structure lords it over the sea towards Denmark. Heading coastwards takes you to a viewpoint of the 8km **Öresund Bridge**, the longest road-and-rail bridge in Europe. There's also access to the Ribban, Malmö's artificial sandy beach.

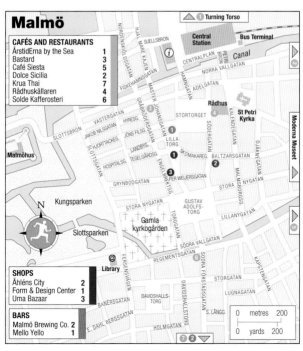

Malmö

CAFÉS AND RESTAURANTS
ÅrstidErna by the Sea	1
Bastard	3
Café Siesta	5
Dolce Sicilia	2
Krua Thai	7
Rådhuskällaren	4
Solde Kafferosteri	6

SHOPS
Åhléns City	2
Form & Design Center	1
Uma Bazaar	3

BARS
Malmö Brewing Co.	2
Mello Yello	1

Shops

Åhléns City

MAP P.107

Södergatan 15 📞 040 24 13 00, 🌐 ahlens.
se. Mon–Fri 10am–8pm, Sat 10am–7pm,
Sun 11am–6pm.

Malmö's glitziest department store,
packed with Swedish designer labels
including Acne and Nudie Jeans.

Form & Design Center

MAP P.107

Lilla Torg 9 📞 040 664 51 50,
🌐 formdesigncenter.com. Tues–Sat
11am–5pm, Sun noon–4pm.

This gallery-café-shop has a lot to
offer including a good selection of
Scandinavian design knick-knacks,
and some handmade items (tea
cosies, candlestick holders and the
like) by local artists.

Uma Bazaar

MAP P.107

Per Wijersgatan 9 📞 040 12 30 85,
🌐 umabazaar.se. Mon–Fri 11am–6pm, Sat
11am–4pm.

Fair Trade shop that sells everything
from Indian pillows and African
carpets to recycled jeans and
wooden watches. Being Swedish it's
all resolutely stylish, organic and
sustainable.

Cafés and restaurants

ÅrstidErna by the Sea

MAP P.107

Dockgatan 1 📞 040 23 34 88,
🌐 arstidernabythesea.se. Mon–Fri lunch
11.30am–1.30pm, Wed–Sat dinner from
5pm.

Large glass-fronted seafood
restaurant located at the marina
in the Western harbour area.
The menu centres on primarily
locally and sustainably sourced

Bastard

produce such as lovely pan-fried cod (175SEK) and a wonderful seafood soup.

Bastard

MAP P.107

Mäster Johansgatan 11 ⊙ **040 12 13 18,** ⓦ **bastardrestaurant.se. Tues–Thurs 5pm–midnight, Fri & Sat 5pm–1am.**

Yes, you read that right. This hip gastropub-style restaurant, run by tattooed young chef Andreas Dahlberg, has brought nose-to-tail dining to Malmö, be it pig cheek, heart, trotters or tongue. Don't miss the *Bastarrdplanka*, a mix of sausages, hams and pâté served on a wooden board. Excellent wines too. Mains from 125SEK.

Café Siesta

MAP P.107

Hjorttackegatan 1 ⊙ **040 611 10 27,** ⓦ **siesta.nu. Tues–Thurs 4–11pm, Fri & Sat 11.30am–1am.**

Terrific little café, popular for brunch on weekends when you can enjoy the likes of smoked salmon smørrebrød (85SEK) and french toast. Evening mains include sea bass with zucchini and grilled lemon (170–235SEK).

Dolce Sicilia

MAP P.107

Drottningtorget 6 ⊙ **040 611 31 10,** ⓦ **dolcesicilia.se. Daily 11am–7pm (closed Mon and after 5.30pm in winter; open till 8.30pm in June and July).**

A proper Italian-run *gelateria* with delicious organic ice cream made fresh every day, as well as coffee and ciabatta. Also a prime people-watching spot.

Krua Thai

MAP P.107

Möllevångstorget 12 ⊙ **040 12 22 87,** ⓦ **kruathai.se. Mon 11am–3pm, Tues–Fri 11am–9pm, Sat & Sun 1–9pm.**

Affordable, authentic Thai food just south of the centre on Möllevångstorget. Pad Thai 89SEK. Unlicensed.

Rådhuskällaren

MAP P.107

Stortorget 2 ⊙ **040 79 020,** ⓦ **radhuskallareni.se. Mon–Fri 11.30am–2pm & 5–11pm, Sat 5–11pm, Sun 3–8pm.**

Historic restaurant in the vaulted cellar of the town hall, serving a good-value lunch buffet (110SEK including salad, cheese and coffee) and a sophisticated à la carte dinner menu featuring meaty mains such as pork tenderloin or cajun fried chicken (from 169SEK).

Solde Kafferosteri

MAP P.107

Regementsgatan 2 ⊙ **046 73 935 77 70,** ⓦ **solde.se. Mon–Fri 7am–6pm, Sat 9am–4pm, Sun 10am–4pm.**

Lovely coffee bar that also sells cakes, sandwiches and fresh roasted beans. Perfectly poured, ethically sourced and organic.

Bars

Malmö Brewing Co

MAP P.107

Bergsgatan 33 ⊙ **040 20 96 85,** ⓦ **malmobrewing.com. Mon–Thurs 4–midnight, Fri & Sun 4pm–3am, Sat noon–3am.**

Sup pale ales, pilsners and porters at the city's only microbrewery, a ten-minute walk south of the old centre. The attached pub is open late and on Fridays and Saturdays you can take a tour of the brewery itself (300SEK).

Mello Yello

MAP P.107

Lilla Torg 1 ⊙ **040 30 45 25,** ⓦ **melloyello. se. Mon–Thurs 3.30pm–1am, Fri 1.30pm–1am, Sat & Sun noon–1am.**

This stylish bar is the best of the bunch on Lilla Torg. The long cocktail list is supplemented by good draught beers including Brooklyn lager. Food ranges from delicious small delicacies (179SEK for five dishes) to excellent seafood.

ACCOMMODATION

Urban House

Accommodation

Hotels do not come cheap in Copenhagen, hovering around the 800–1200kr (£90–130/€110–160) mark for an average double room in high season (late June to early September). Those close to the sights of Tivoli and the Inner City (Indre By) are particularly expensive, while the Vesterbro area is the city's budget hotel district with Helgolandsgade in particular lined with more affordable options. Facilities offered at most places are ultra-modern, boasting fabulous design and eco-conscious features in true Danish style. The prices listed below are based on two adults sharing the cheapest en-suite double room in high season inclusive of tax (25 percent). If breakfast costs extra we have indicated this in the review. Online discounts and opting for a shared bathroom can reduce prices significantly.

Tivoli and Rådhuspladsen

CAB-INN CITY MAP P.25, POCKET MAP B14. Mitchellsgade 14 ☎ 33 46 16 16, ⊛ cabinn.com. Modern budget hotel around the corner from Central Station and a stone's throw from Tivoli, Cab-Inn's main forte – apart from its compact and super-functional cabin-style rooms – is its central yet relatively quiet location away from the hubbub of Vesterbro. Rooms sleep up to three people. Part of a larger chain with hotels in Frederiksberg (Vodroffsvej 55 and Danasvej 22) and another one in Ørestaden (Arne Jakobsens Allé 2) designed by Daniel Libeskind. Breakfast 90kr. **675kr**

HOTEL NIMB MAP P.25, POCKET MAP A13. Bernstorffsgade 5 ☎ 88 70 00 00, ⊛ hotel.nimb.dk. Fairy-tale hotel located upstairs in Tivoli's Moorish-inspired Nimb building from 1909. With just fourteen individually decorated extravagant rooms this is Copenhagen's original boutique hotel. Features include open fireplaces, antique wooden furniture and sweeping views of the gardens. *Hotel Nimb's* opulence encompasses in-room massage (for 1300kr an hour) and a private chauffeur service (1100kr to be picked up at the airport). **30000kr**

HOTEL TWENTYSEVEN MAP P.25, POCKET MAP B13. Løngangstræde 27 ☎ 70 27 56 27, ⊛ firsthotels.com. Good-value designer hotel slap bang in the city centre and a minute's walk from the Rådhus (whose bells toll every fifteen minutes until midnight and from 7am in the morning, so worth bearing in mind if you're a light sleeper). With spacious modern rooms and a popular courtyard where cocktails from the hotel's *Honey Ryder* cocktail bar can be devoured. Breakfast 100kr. **1080kr**

PALACE HOTEL MAP P.25, POCKET MAP B12. Rådhuspladsen 57 ☎ 33 14 40 50, ⊛ palacehotelcopenhagen.com. Wonderful Art Nouveau hotel from 1910 located next door to the Rådhus. A recent refurbishment has reinstated its original decor, featuring lovely details such as George Jensen silver door handles and abstract artwork on the walls. During its heyday many a Hollywood star stayed here including the likes of Audrey Hepburn and Gregory Peck. Although restored to their original appearance, rooms have been totally modernized with comfy beds and luxurious bathrooms. Breakfast included. **1630kr**

RADISSON BLU ROYAL HOTEL MAP P.25, POCKET MAP A13. Hammerichsgade 1 ☎ 33

42 60 00, ⓦ radissonblu.com/royalhotel-copenhagen. The *Royal Hotel* is an Arne Jakobsen masterpiece and a prominent example of Danish modernist architecture. A twenty-two-storey rectangular grey and green structure, the hotel is today graced with his furniture throughout, including the famous Swan, Egg, and Drop chairs which were designed specifically for the hotel. Although modern luxury abounds, the hotel today also has a funky time-warped feeling, not least as you step into the 1960s lobby. For the full retro experience book the Arne Jacobsen suite (Room 606) which comes in at an eye-watering 5500kr a night. Breakfast 300kr. **1695kr**

THE SQUARE MAP P.25, POCKET MAP A12. Rådhuspladsen 14 ☏ 33 38 12 00, ⓦ thesquarecopenhagen.com. Stylish, smart hotel that is conveniently located for easy access to Tivoli and the downtown shopping district. Housed in a former office block, the minimalist rooms – spread over five floors – have been tastefully decorated and come with all of the required mod cons discreetly tucked away. The breakfast restaurant on the sixth floor offers some great views of the city. Breakfast 178kr. **1228kr**

Strøget and the Inner City

D'ANGLETERRE MAP P.32, POCKET MAP E11. Kongens Nytorv 34 ☏ 33 12 00 95, ⓦ dangleterre.com. This prestigious hotel dating from 1755 is Copenhagen's answer to *The Ritz* in London; hotel of choice for anyone who's anyone, from rock stars to US presidents. Offering classic elegance, with modern Danish design kept to a minimum (although you will find Bang & Olufsen TV screens above the bath tubs), the hotel encompasses a five-hundred-square-metre luxurious spa and fitness centre, a grand restaurant, and a new champagne bar with

over 160 different champanges on the menu. Breakfast 570kr. **3000kr**

HOTEL SANKT PETRI MAP P.32, POCKET MAP B11. Krystalgade 22 ☏ 33 45 91 00, ⓦ sktpetri.com. Ultra-stylish design hotel housed in a former five-storey functionalistic department store. The spacious rooms have dark parquet flooring and sleek Scandinavian furniture such as the super-comfortable Jensen bed. The hotel is full of business travellers during the week; you can usually pick up competitive deals at weekends. Breakfast 200kr. **1590kr**

Nyhavn and Frederiksstaden

71 NYHAVN MAP P.52, POCKET MAP F11. Nyhavn 71 ☏ 33 43 62 00, ⓦ 71nyhavnhotel.com. Two interconnected converted warehouses overlooking Inderhavnen and next door to the city's new playhouse, *71 Nyhavn* is a charming place to stay. Although it is slightly on the small side, the hotel's magnificent location easily makes up for this slight shortfall. Superior rooms feature pretty French doors opening onto a balcony. Primarily a business hotel, there are some good deals to be had during summer. Breakfast buffet 170kr. **1419kr**

ADMIRAL HOTEL MAP P.52, POCKET MAP F11. Toldbodgade 24 ☏ 33 74 14 14, ⓦ admiralhotel.dk. Romantic waterfront hotel in a vast converted warehouse from 1787 with lots of its original features still intact such as vaulted brick ceilings and enormous wooden beams. There are 300 rooms spread over six floors, each with its own unique charm; a sea view will cost extra. Breakfast is served in the downstairs restaurant *Salt* (see page 58) which is

Booking ahead

In order to get the lowest room rate book well in advance or try one of the many online booking sites. If you do arrive without a reservation the city tourist office should be able to help at their offices in the airport and on Vesterbrogade (see page 125) and online at ⓦ visitcopenhagen.com.

also a good bet for other meals, or simply to hang out in its waterfront café section. Breakfast 170kr. **1685kr**

BABETTE GULDSMEDEN MAP P.52, POCKET MAP G6. Bredgade 78 ☎ 33 14 15 00, Ⓦ guldsmedenhotels.com. Formerly the *Hotel Esplanaden*, the Guldsmeden hotel group have added a touch of luxury to this old building, which overlooks Churchill Parken and Kastellet. There's a rooftop spa and brasserie for real indulgence. Breakfast 225kr. **1295kr**

SØMANDSHJEMMET BETHEL MAP P.52, POCKET MAP F11. Nyhavn 22 ☎ 33 13 03 70, Ⓦ hotel-bethel.dk. A former hostel for Icelandic sailors, *Bethel*'s superb location overlooking Nyhavn Kanal and the bars and restaurants on the opposite bank can hardly be bettered. Bearing this in mind, the somewhat dated but perfectly comfortable, clean and tidy rooms are excellent value. Ask at reception for a tour of the sailor's church round the back if that's what floats your boat. **845kr**

Rosenborg and around

IBSEN MAP P.62, POCKET MAP A10. Vendersgade 23 ☎ 33 13 19 13, Ⓦ arthurhotels.dk/ibsens-hotel. Arty hotel situated on a Nansensgade street corner with bright and airy rooms spread over five floors in two interconnected nineteenth-century apartment buildings. Works by local artists (some for sale) are on display throughout the hotel, and the management even accept art for part payment of rooms (see Ⓦ artmoney.org). Discounted access to Ni'Mat spa next door for 250kr. Breakfast 155kr. **1530kr**

JØRGENSEN MAP P.62, POCKET MAP A10. Rømersgade 11 ☎ 33 13 81 86, Ⓦ hoteljoergensen.dk. Superb value, slightly run-down hotel-cum-hostel a stone's throw from Torvehallerne. housing a range of rooms in different shapes and sizes, a few with en-suite bathrooms. The tightly packed dorms sleep six to ten and there is no internet access. Breakfast buffet 45kr (included if you book a private room). Dorm beds 175kr, doubles **750kr**

Christianshavn and Holmen

CPH LIVING MAP P.72, POCKET MAP D14. Langebrogade 1C ☎ 61 60 85 46, Ⓦ cphliving.com. Absolutely gorgeous hotel boat with twelve identical smartly furnished rooms all facing Christian IV's red-brick brew-house on the opposite bank. Reception is unstaffed and you need an access code to get in, which is given to you when you pay for the room. The reception area doubles as a help-yourself breakfast buffet, which you can eat on the sundeck while taking in the fine views and fresh sea air. Moored next to it is the restaurant boat *Viva* (see page 76). **1460kr**

Vesterbro and Frederiksberg

ABSALON MAP P.80, POCKET MAP D8. Helgolandsgade 15 ☎ 33 31 43 44, Ⓦ absalon-hotel.dk. Large good-value family-run hotel that has recently been refurbished with en-suite facilities and a fresh, bright decor in the colourful rooms, some of which can accommodate families of up to four. **1100kr**

ANSGAR MAP P.80, POCKET MAP A14. Colbjørnsensgade 29 ☎ 33 21 21 96, Ⓦ ansgarhotel.dk. Small, friendly recently renovated family hotel in what used to be the dodgy red-light district of Vesterbro. The no-frills tidy rooms are superb value and the price includes a lavish breakfast buffet which in summer is served on an outdoor terrace. **900kr**

CITY HOTEL NEBO MAP P.80, POCKET MAP D8. Istedgade 6 ☎ 33 21 12 17, Ⓦ nebo.dk. Age-old Danish Mission hotel whose profits all go to a Vesterbro homeless shelter behind Central Station. Rooms are nothing to write home about but perfectly pleasant and clean, some with en-suite bathroom, others sharing shower and toilet in the corridor. Breakfast buffet 75kr. **800kr**

COPENHAGEN ISLAND MAP P.80, POCKET MAP D9. Kalvebod Brygge 53 ☎ 33

38 96 00, Ⓦ **copenhagenisland.dk**. The Kim Utzon-designed *Copenhagen Island* is as sleek as it gets. With wonderful large windows looking out to the Copencabana harbour pool just outside, you could be excused for thinking that you're on a seaside holiday. Inside the stylish rooms are beautifully furnished with modern Danish design and top of the range electronics. In the hotel basement there's a fitness centre with steam bath and sauna. Breakfast 150kr. **1195kr**

GULDSMEDEN AXEL MAP P.80, POCKET MAP D8. Helgolandsgade 8 Ⓣ 33 31 32 66, Ⓦ **hotelguldsmeden.com/axel**. Among the city's most appealing boutique hotels with beautiful Balinese-inspired decor and superb attention to detail. This is where the supermodels come to stay and you're likely to feel like one of them after a couple of days, your every whim being catered for by the super-attentive staff. Given the level of pampering, all this comes at a very reasonable price. Breakfast buffet 225kr. **1490kr**

GULDSMEDEN BERTRAMS MAP P.80, POCKET MAP C8. Vesterbrogade 107 Ⓣ 70 20 81 07, Ⓦ **hotelguldsmeden.com/bertrams**. Another of the Guldsmeden (Dragonfly) boutique hotel chain (see above), this one styling French colonial decor with wonderful dark wooden furniture and the occasional fake fur laying around. Not as large as the *Axel* branch, *Bertrams* has a slightly more personable and intimate feel, not least as the intimidating fashion-week types don't tend to stay here. Breakfast 155kr. No under-18s. **1490kr**

HOTEL CENTRAL & CAFÉ MAP P.80, POCKET MAP C8. Tullinsgade 1 Ⓣ 33 21 00 95, Ⓦ **centralhotelogcafe.dk**. Set above an appropriately tiny (five-seat) coffeeshop and once inhabited by a cobbler, this one-room spot definitely earns its billing as "the smallest hotel in the world". A bed, bathroom and flat-screen TV are squeezed into the twelve-metre-square room that nevertheless beckons with some real attention to detail and olde-worlde charm. **1800kr**

LØVEN MAP P.80, POCKET MAP D8. Vesterbrogade 30 Ⓣ 33 79 67 20,

Ⓦ **loevenhotel.dk**. A basic hotel on noisy Vesterbrogade, the real benefit of *Løven* is its excellent value and the lively and very helpful owner who runs it as a tight ship. The plain rooms come with up to five beds, some sharing facilities, others en suite. Though there's no breakfast on offer, there's a fully fitted kitchen should you wish to self-cater. Wi-fi is only available in the kitchen. **590kr**

SAGA HOTEL MAP P.80, POCKET MAP D8. Colbjørnsensgade 18–20 Ⓣ 33 24 49 44, Ⓦ **sagahotel.dk**. In the once grotty red-light district of Vesterbro, family-run *Saga* is today one of the city's really good budget options and popular with backpackers who've had their fill of rowdy and impersonal hostels. The sparsely decorated rooms sleeping up to five mostly share facilities although there are also a few en-suite rooms. Filling breakfasts are served on the second floor in a cosy dining area. **950kr**

SCT THOMAS MAP P.80, POCKET MAP C8. Frederiksberg Allé 7 Ⓣ 33 21 64 64, Ⓦ **hotelsctthomas.dk**. Popular small Frederiksberg hotel housed in a nineteenth-century apartment block not far from lively Værnedamsvej and offering simple uncluttered rooms. The buffet breakfast, served in the newly excavated basement, is one of the best in town. Free internet only in the lobby. **795kr**

WAKE UP COPENHAGEN MAP P.80, POCKET MAP D9. Carsten Niebuhrs Gade 11 Ⓣ 44 80 00 00, Ⓦ **wakeupcopenhagen.com**. Super-efficient and slightly impersonal, this brand-new budget hotel on the edge of Vesterbro overlooks the railway line to one side and Inner Havnen to the other. Spread over nine floors, the 500-odd a/c rooms verge on the small side but feel perfectly adequate thanks to the clever design and layout created by architect Kim Utzon. Larger rooms and rooms with a better view cost more. Breakfast 90kr. **850kr**

ZLEEP HOTEL CENTRUM MAP P.80, POCKET MAP D9. Helgolandsgade 14 Ⓣ 70 23 56 35, Ⓦ **zleephotels.com**. No-frills accommodation a stone's throw from Central Station, this really is as Spartan as

Our top places to stay

For a damn-the-cost weekend: *D'Angleterre* see page 113
For romance: *Hotel Central & Café* see page 115
For luxury on a budget: *Hotel Twentyseven* see page 112, *Guldsmeden Bertrams* see page 115
For peace and quiet: *Copenhagen Island* see page 114
For Danish design: *Radisson Blu Royal Hotel* see page 112
Location, location: *CPH Living* see page 114
Watching the pennies: *Løven* see page 115, *Copenhagen Downtown* see page 116

it gets. Hence the very reasonable prices, particularly if you book far in advance. Part of a wider Zleep concept chain, the hotel provides largely self-service accommodation with food and drink available from vending machines – although the basic breakfast buffet (99kr) is manned. Rooms sleep up to four. **499kr**

Nørrebro and Østerbro

AVENUE MAP P.88, POCKET MAP C6. **Åboulevard 29** ⓣ **35 37 31 11,** ⓦ **avenuehotel.dk.** Out from the centre on the border between Nørrebro and Frederiksberg, *Avenue* has three key things going for it: the spacious classically furnished rooms, free parking, and very reasonable rates. It also has the added bonus of not being part of a chain, which gives it that personable vibe that makes you feel right at home. **1020kr**

HOTEL RYE MAP P.90, POCKET MAP E4. **Ryesgade 115** ⓣ **35 26 52 10,** ⓦ **rye115.com.** Homely *Hotel Rye* is a brilliant option away from the city centre yet near the lively lake area of Østerbro and the tranquil Fælledparken. Housed in a former care home, the sixteen highly individualized rooms are spread over the second and third floors of an apartment building. All have shared bathroom in the hall (you are provided with a kimono and slippers for nocturnal visits). Outside the back yard is equipped with a play area for kids, and in the cosy dining area freshly baked rolls are available with breakfast every morning. **900kr**

Hostels

Copenhagen has some excellent hostels that can often rival budget hotels in terms of value and style. Many offer private doubles, twins and triples as well as the usual dorm rooms. Be aware that the latter are often packed with rowdy Swedish students during the summer holidays and availability can be an issue at these times. Danhostel (ⓦ danhostel.dk) which runs two of the hostels below charges a one-off membership fee of 70kr if you don't hold a Hostelling International card. Note that *Jørgensen* (see page 114) also offers dorm beds.

COPENHAGEN DOWNTOWN MAP P.32, POCKET MAP C12. **Vandkunsten 5** ⓣ **70 23 21 10,** ⓦ **copenhagendowntown.com.** Though affiliated to Danhostel, *Copenhagen Downtown* has a hip, independent feel with guests sprawling on bean bags out onto the pavement, and a cool retro Scandinavian design. The location right next to some superb music venues and a plethora of watering holes is also hard to beat. Rooms are on the smallish side sleeping two to ten people in bunk beds, usually with shared bathroom, but everything is clean and tidy and the vibe energetic. Breakfast 70kr. **Dorm beds 210kr, doubles 660kr**

DANHOSTEL CITY MAP P.25, POCKET MAP C14. **H.C Andersens Boulevard 50** ⓣ **70 88 39 71,** ⓦ **danhostelcopenhagencity.dk.** Modern five-star hostel housed in Denmark's first high-rise building, dating from 1955. Encompassing over a thousand beds in four-, six-, eight- and ten-bed rooms spread over sixteen floors it offers wonderful views over Copenhagen. Add the interior design by GUBI and facilities such as a bar-café in the lobby and games room in the basement and you could be forgiven for thinking that you're staying at a modern hotel albeit one with bunk beds. Breakfast 75kr. **Dorm beds 195kr, doubles 615kr**

GENERATOR MAP P.62, POCKET MAP D10. Adelgade 5–7 ☎ 78 77 54 00, ⓦ generatorhostels.com. Part of a Europe-wide chain of funky hostels, this one is housed in an apartment block designed by Phillipe Starck. It's one of the best places to stay in town if you're young and adventurous, but like your creature

comforts. All rooms come with en-suite bathrooms and range from twin-bed doubles to (pink) female dorms sleeping six and mixed dorms sleeping eight. The hostel also offers plenty of places to chill out including a large outdoor terrace and a spacious lounge/bar boasting an enormous TV. Breakfast 75kr. **Dorm beds 250kr, doubles 720k**

URBAN HOUSE MAP P.80, POCKET MAP D8. Colbjørnsensgade 5–11 ☎ 33 23 29 29, ⓦ urbanhouse.me. This trendy hostel/ hotel opened in 2015 with 950 beds in 225 rooms. Dorms and private rooms (sleep 1–4 people), plus an in-house bike shop and tattoo studio. Breakfast 75kr. **Dorms 175kr, doubles 750kr**

ESSENTIALS

Parked-up in Christianshavns

Arrival

However you arrive in Copenhagen you'll find yourself within easy reach of the city centre. Copenhagen Airport is just a few kilometres to the southeast, on the edge of the island of Amager, while almost all trains and buses deposit you near the city's main transport hub, Central Station.

By air

Getting into the city from **Copenhagen Airport** (ⓦ cph.dk), 11km from the city in the suburb of Kastrup, couldn't be easier: one of Europe's fastest airport-to-city rail lines runs directly to Central Station (roughly every 10min; 14min; 38kr). In addition, the metro (every 4–6min during the day, every 15–20min midnight–7am) links the airport with Christianshavn (12min), Kongens Nytorv (13min) and Nørreport (15min) stations (all 38kr) in the centre. Copenhagen Airport is in Zone 3. A taxi to the centre costs about 250–300kr – there's a rank outside the arrivals hall.

You can pick up free maps from the helpful information desk in sleek Terminal 3 (daily 6.10am–11pm). They also sell Copenhagen Cards (see page 121). The airport has two late-opening banks (daily 6am–10pm), lots of ATMs, free wi-fi throughout, 72-hour luggage storage lockers (see page 123), numerous car rental agencies and a post office. The stylish *Hilton Hotel*, connected to the airport by a pedestrian walkway, is a good place to kill some time – their lobby bar is equipped with arrival and departure screens.

Buses from small **Malmö Airport** in Sweden (ⓦ swedavia.com/malmo; see page 107) are integrated with flight arrivals. Some 60km east of Copenhagen, it has retained its role as a hub for budget flights to the city. The one-hour bus journey with Gråhundsbus (ⓦ graahundbus.dk; 120kr) skirts around Malmö itself before crossing the magnificent Öresund Bridge (see page 107), reason enough in itself to opt for the cheaper airfare option.

By bus and train

All buses and trains to Copenhagen arrive at or near **Central Station** (in Danish, Hovedbanegården or København H), the city's main transport hub, from where there are excellent connections to virtually every part of the city via bus or local train – and as from 2019 also a new metro circular line (see opposite). The station also has an array of shops, a foreign-exchange bureau (daily 8am–9pm), places to eat and, downstairs, left-luggage lockers (see page 123). The national train company, DSB, has a travel agency and information centre just inside the main entrance off Vesterbrogade (Mon–Fri 7am–8pm, Sat & Sun 8am–6pm; ☎ 70 13 14 15, ⓦ dsb.dk) and an easy-to-use ticket machine in the hallway (daily 4.30am–2.40am).

Eurolines coaches from around Europe stop behind the station on Ingerslevgade, across from DGI-byen. Buses from Malmö airport stop in front of *Plaza Hotel* next to the station.

Getting around

The best way to explore Copenhagen is either to walk or cycle: the inner city is compact, much of the central area pedestrianized, and there's a comprehensive network of excellent bike paths. For travelling further afield, there's an integrated network of buses, metros, S-Tog (urban rapid transit) and local trains.

Tickets

All city transport operates on a **zonal system** encompassing the metro, trains and buses. The city centre and immediate area, as you'd expect, are in zones 1 and 2. The cheapest ticket (**billet**) costs 24kr and is valid for one hour's travel within any two zones, with unlimited transfers between buses and trains. The excellent value **City Pass**, available for 24 hours (160kr), 48 hours (300kr), 72 hours (400kr), 96 hours (500kr) and 120 hours (600kr), is valid on all transport to as far away as Helsingør and Roskilde, as well as night buses and all public transport to and from the airport (🌐 copenhagencitypass.com). Finally, if you're planning on visiting lots of museums and attractions, the Copenhagen Card (see box) also includes free transport.

Tickets can be bought on board buses or at train stations, while 24-hour tickets are only available at bus or train stations and HT Kortsalg kiosks. Route maps can be picked up free at stations, and most free city maps include bus lines and a diagram of the S-Tog and metro network. For more information see 🌐 dinoffentligetransport.dk

The metro

Copenhagen's fast and efficient underground **metro system** (🌐 m.dk) circumvents the Central Station in a "U" shape, connecting the island of Amager and Copenhagen airport with west Copenhagen via Christianshavn and Kongens Nytorv. The metro's M1 and M2 lines cross the S-Tog and regional trains at Nørreport, Flintholm and Vanløse. The new City Circle (M3) line integrates more effectively with the S-Tog system, and crosses the M1 and M2 lines at Hovedbanegården and Østerport. Metro stations are marked by a large red underlined "M" painted onto aluminium pillars.

S-Tog and regular trains

The **S-Tog** rapid transit service (🌐 dsb.dk) is laid out in a huge "U" shape and covers the whole Copenhagen metropolitan area. Six of its seven lines stop at Central Station, with the others circling the centre. Each line has a letter and is also colour-coded on route maps. Stations are marked by red hexagonal signs with a yellow "S" inside them.

Regular national trains are run by the **Danish State Railway** (DSB; 🌐 dsb.dk) and among other towns connect the city to Helsingør and Roskilde, calling at Østerport and Nørreport stations and some suburban destinations on the way.

The Copenhagen Card

If you plan to do lots of sightseeing, you might want to buy a **Copenhagen Card**. Valid for 24, 48, 72 or 120 hours (399kr/599kr/739kr/989kr), it covers public transport (including Helsingør and Roskilde) and gives free (or discounted) entry to most museums. This can save a lot of money – especially since it can also give you twenty- to fifty-percent off car rental, ferry rides and theatre tickets. You can either book the card in advance online at 🌐 copenhagencard.com or pick one up on arrival at the airport, visitor centre or Central Station.

Buses

The city's **bus** network (⊕ moviatrafik. dk) is more comprehensive than the S-Tog system and can be a more convenient way to get around once you get the hang of finding the stops – marked by yellow placards on signposts – and as long as you avoid the rush hour (7–9am & 5–6pm). The vast majority stop at Rådhuspladsen next to Tivoli. Buses with an "S" suffix only make limited stops, offering a faster service – check they make the stop you require before you get on. Buses with an "A" suffix indicate that the bus runs frequently. All buses have a small electronic board above the driver's seat displaying both the zone you're currently in and the time – so there's no excuse for not having a valid ticket. A skeletal **night-bus** (natdrift) runs once or twice an hour (fares remain the same). Night-bus numbers always end with "N".

Harbour buses

A cheaper way to experience Copenhagen from the waterfront than a canal tour (see box opposite), yellow **harbour "buses"** sail along the harbour between Nordre Toldbod (near the Little Mermaid) and the Royal Library, stopping six times and costing the same as a normal bus fare. Services (daily every 20min about 7am–7pm) are cancelled when the harbour is frozen.

Cycling

If the weather's good, the best way to see Copenhagen is to do as the locals do and get on your bike. The superb, city-wide cycle lanes make **cycling** very safe and bikes can be taken on S-Tog trains (free of charge) through any number of zones. Lights are mandatory at night (you'll be stopped and fined if the police catch you without them). Despite a recent campaign to promote wearing helmets few locals do so. You can usually **rent bikes** through your hotel or hostel (around 100kr/day). Otherwise try Københavns Cyklebørs, Gothersgade 157, Indre By (Mon–Fri 10am–5.30pm, Sat & Sun 10am–2pm; ☎ 33 14 07 17, ⊕ cykelboersen.dk; 90kr/day, 450kr/week, 300kr deposit); Pedal Atleten, Oslo Plads 9, next to Østerport Station (Mon–Fri 8am–6pm, Sat 10am–3pm; ☎ 70 70 75 13, ⊕ pedalatleten.dk; 100kr/day, 375kr/week, 500kr deposit); or Baisikeli, Ingerslevsgade 103 (daily 10am–4/6pm; ☎ 26 70 02 29, ⊕ baisikeli.dk; from 50kr for six hours, 270kr/week, 200kr deposit).

Taxis

Taxis are plentiful, but with a flat starting fare of 24kr, then 15kr per kilometre (19kr after 4pm and at weekends), they're only worth taking in a group. There's a handy rank outside Central Station; you can also book with Taxa (☎ 35 35 35 35) or hail one in the street – the green "Fri" sign on top shows it's available. Rickshaw-styled **cycle taxis** (April–Oct; ☎ 45 26 18 58 00, ⊕ rickshaw.dk), carrying a maximum of two people, operate a flat starting fare of 40kr if you flag them down on the street, then charge 4kr per minute.

Directory A–Z

Addresses

The street name is always written before the house number, which is followed by the apartment number or floor the apartment is on, followed by the side the apartment is at (t.h. – to the right as you come up the stairs, and t.v. – to the left). So, Læssøesgade 16 3 t.h., means the third-floor apartment to the right, in

Emergency numbers

Dial ☎ 112 for police, fire or ambulance.

building number 16 on Læssøesgade. The city is divided into postal districts consisting of four digits followed by the area so Indre By is Kbh K preceded by a four-digit number; Østerbro is Kbh Ø, Nørrebro Kbh N, Vesterbro Kbh V, Amager Kbh S and Frederiksberg Fred. After the completion of the bridge across to Sweden the city of Malmö is jokingly called Kbh M.

Cinema
International blockbusters are screened at Imperial (Ved Vesterport 4 ☎ 70 13 12 11, ⊛ nfbio.dk/imperial). More alternative films are shown at Grand Teatret (Mikkel Bryggersgade 8 ☎ 33 15 16 11, ⊛ grandteatret.dk) and Vester Vov Vov (Absalonsgade 5 ☎ 33 24 42 00, ⊛ vestervovvov.dk).

Crime
Copenhagen has an extremely low crime rate. Keep an eye on your cash and passport and you should have little reason to visit the **police**. If you do, you'll find them courteous and usually able to speak English. The central police station is at Polititorvet 14 (☎ 33 14 88 88).

Electricity
The Danish electricity supply runs at 220–240V, 50Hz AC; sockets generally require a two-pin plug. Visitors from the UK will need an adaptor; visitors from outside the EU may need a transformer.

Embassies and consulates
Australia Dampfærgevej 26, 2nd floor ☎ 70 26 36 76; Canada Kristen Bernikowsgade 1 ☎ 33 48 32 00; Ireland Østbanegade 21 ☎ 35 47 32 00; South Africa Gammel Vartov 8, Hellerup ☎ 39 18 01 85; UK Kastelsvej 36–40

☎ 35 44 52 00; US Dag Hammerskjölds Allé 24 ☎ 33 41 71 00.

Health
There are **24-hour emergency departments** at Bispebjerg Hospital, Bispebjerg Bakke 23 (☎ 38 63 50 00) and Hvidovre Hospital, Kettegårds Alle 30 (☎ 38 62 38 62). If you need a **doctor**, call ☎ 70 13 00 41 (after 4pm or on weekends) or you can call 1813 for any emergencies. For **dental emergencies**, contact Tandlægevagten, Oslo Plads 14 ☎ 70 25 00 41 (Mon–Fri 8am–9.30pm, Sat & Sun 10am–noon, 8–9.30pm).

The city's two main 24-hour **pharmacies** are Steno Apotek, Vesterbrogade 6C in front of Central Station (☎ 33 14 82 66) and Sønderbro Apotek, Amagerbrogade 158, Amager (☎ 32 58 01 40).

Internet
Copenhagen has plenty of wireless hubs in cafés and bars and on trains. Most hotels and hostels – and even some campsites – offer wi-fi (most for free), and access is also available **free** at libraries (though not the Royal Library).

Left luggage
The DSB Garderobe office downstairs in Central Station **stores luggage** for 70/80kr per item per day and has lockers (Mon–Sat 5.30am–1am, Sun 6am–1am; 70kr/80kr for 24hr). Copenhagen airport's left-luggage facility, in Parking House P4 across the road from terminal 2 (open 24hr), has small and large lockers for 60kr (4 hours) or 80kr (24 hour) and 80kr (4 hours) or 120kr (24 hours) per day respectively (4 hours to max 7 days).

LGBTQ Copenhagen

Copenhagen is one of the world's top gay destinations. Attitudes are very tolerant and there is a lively LGBTQ scene enjoyed by many straight people, too. The Copenhagen Pride festival (see page 126) is a particularly great time to experience gay Copenhagen. Check out Ⓦ copenhagen.gaycities.com to see what's on.

Lost property

The police department's **lost-property** office is at Slotsherrensvej 113, Vanløse ☎ 38 74 88 22. For items lost on a bus, contact the bus information office on ☎ 70 15 70 00 (Mon–Fri 9am–2pm); for items lost on a train or S-Tog, there's a lost luggage office at Central Station (Mon–Fri 8am–8pm, Sat & Sun 10am–5pm) or contact them on ☎ 24 68 09 60 (Mon–Fri 10am–1pm); for lost property at Copenhagen Airport go to Terminal 3 or look online at Ⓦ missingx.com.

Money

The Danish currency is the **krone** (plural kroner), made up of 100 øre, and comes in notes of 1000kr, 500kr, 200kr, 100kr and 50kr, and coins of 20kr, 10kr, 5kr, 2kr, 1kr, 50øre. At the time of writing, the exchange rate was approximately 10.10kr to the pound, 7.45kr to the euro and 6.70kr to the US dollar. For the latest rates, go to Ⓦ xe.com.

PIN codes are always required when paying by card.

Opening hours

Shops tend to open Mon–Thurs 10am–6pm, Fri 10am–7pm, Sat 10am–4pm, Sun noon–4pm but shops in the centre of town tend to have longer hours. Most offices are open Mon–Fri 9am–4/4.30pm.

Phones

You should be able to use your **mobile phone** though it may be cheaper to buy a Danish SIM card. For 99kr, you'll get a Danish number plus about forty minutes of domestic calls. The most commonly used network is TDC, but coverage with Telemore, Telenor and others is just as good. SIM cards and credit can be bought in supermarkets, kiosks and phone shops.

Calling Denmark from abroad, the **international code** is ☎ 45. For **collect international calls** from Denmark dial ☎ 80 30 40 00 – instructions for this "Country Direct" system are in phone booths (in English), call ☎ 80 60 40 50 for free assistance.

Post

It can be hard to find a post office these days, although there is still one inside Central Station (Mon–Fri 9am–7pm, Sat noon–4pm). Mail under 50g costs 25kr (within Europe) or 30kr

Public holidays

Denmark observes most religious holidays and moveable feasts. On the following days, expect all banks and most shops to be closed, and check the websites of attractions. Easter is a five-day holiday, followed by a number of single religious holidays up until Whitsuntide.

December 31 New Year; **January 1** New Year's Day; Maundy Thursday; Good Friday; Easter Sunday; Easter Monday; *Store Bededay* (Day of Repentance and Prayer, 4th Friday after Easter); Ascension Day (6th Thurs after Easter); Whitsun (Sun & Mon, 7 weeks after Easter); **December 24** Christmas Eve; **December 25** Christmas Day; **December 26** Boxing Day.

Guided Tours

As well as these operators, the Copenhagen Visitor Centre on Vesterbrogade (see below) has a long list of English-language guided walking tours many of which are free.

Bike Copenhagen with Mike ☎ 26 39 56 88, ⓦ bikecopenhagenwithmike.dk. Cycle tours to Vesterbro, Amalienborg, the Little Mermaid, Christiania and much more, led by the knowledgeable and charismatic Mike. No booking required. 300kr including bike. Cash only.

Copenhagen Sightseeing Tours ⓦ sightseeing.dk. A variety of bus tours (including hop-on hop-off routes which cover stretches by canal boat) with multilingual headphone commentary. From 175kr.

Copenhagen Food Tours ☎ 50 12 36 45, ⓦ copenhagen.foodtours.eu. Three-hour (Tues–Sat 11am, 850kr) and four-hour (Mon–Sat 10am; 900kr) walking tours sampling tasters from the latest movers and shakers on the Danish food scene. The tasters along the way add up to a full-blown meal, so best to arrive hungry. Tours start and end at Torvehallerne.

Kajak Ole ☎ 40 50 40 06, ⓦ kajakole.dk. Kayak tours (April–Oct) giving a unique view of the city from the water. Choose between a 90min paddle around Christianshavn to a 3hr circumnavigation of Slotsholmen. From 345kr including a canalside drink. Tours start from in front of *Færge Caféen*.

Netto-Bådene ☎ 32 54 41 02, ⓦ havnerundfart.dk. Excellent-value one-hour canal tours departing from Holmens Kirke and taking in Nyhavn, Holmen, Nyholm, Amalienborg Palace and the Little Mermaid. 60kr.

(rest of the world). You can buy stamps from most newsagents.

Smoking

Smoking is banned in all public buildings and restaurants as well as on station concourses and platforms. Bars and cafés under forty square metres which do not serve fresh food may still allow smoking.

Time

Denmark is one hour ahead of GMT, six hours ahead of US Eastern Standard Time, and nine ahead of US Pacific Standard Time.

Tipping

Service is included on all restaurant, hotel and taxi bills, so unless you feel you've been given exceptionally good service, tipping is not necessary.

Tourist information

The Copenhagen Visitor Centre (Mon–Fri 9am–4pm, Sat 9am–2pm; ☎ 70 22 24 42, ⓦ visitcopenhagen.com), across the road from the Central Station at Vesterbrogade 4A, offers maps, general information and accommodation reservations, along with free accommodation-booking terminals.

Travellers with disabilities

Copenhagen is a model city for travellers with disabilities: wheelchair access, facilities and help are generally available at hotels, hostels, museums and public places. To see whether a place caters for travellers with disabilities, check the website ⓦ godadgang.dk or contact the tourist office at ⓦ visitcopenhagen.com.

Travelling with children

Copenhagen is a very child-friendly city with reserved children's pram areas on buses and trains, and children's menus and high seats available at most restaurants. The low level of traffic and many pedestrianized streets also make for a stress-free visit with kids.

Festivals and events

Copenhagen Beer Festival

Long weekend in May ⓦ ale.dk
A new and already very popular festival housed in the recently reopened TAP1 bottling hall in the Carlsberg area, featuring over a thousand different beers from around the world.

Copenhagen Carnival

Whitsun weekend ⓦ karneval-kbh.dk
A mini Rio of samba and colourful costumes along Strøget and Købmagergade which culminates in all-night partying at Fælledparken supposedly allowing you to see the Whitsun sun "dance" as it rises in the early hours of the morning.

Sankt Hans Aften

Midsummer's eve ⓦ visitcopenhagen.com
Bonfires and traditional Danish folksongs at various locations along the Copenhagen coast. Check the tourist board website for locations and times.

Roskilde Festival

Last week of June or first week of July (see page 99) ⓦ roskilde-festival.dk
Four-day Glastonbury-style music festival in the outskirts of Roskilde preceded by four days' warm-up in the camping area.

Copenhagen Jazz Festival

First or second week of July ⓦ jazz.dk
Local and international jazz stars – young and old – take over the city's music stages and venues, as well as many outside spaces, making it Europe's biggest jazz event. With loads of free gigs the entire city seems to be swinging to all sorts of jazz imaginable.

Copenhagen Pride

One week in July or August ⓦ copenhagenpride.dk
Superb week of gay events focused on the area around Frederiksholms Kanal and culminating in the flamboyant and colourful Gay Pride Parade which makes its way through the centre of town on the festival Saturday.

Copenhagen Cooking

Last ten days of August ⓦ copenhagen cooking.dk
Riding on the Nordic cuisine popularity wave, over one hundred events across the city hosted by many of the city's famous chefs give you an opportunity to sample some of the amazing creations.

CPH:PIX

Eighteen-day film festival in October/November ⓦ cphpix.dk
The city's premier film festival which features a wide range of Danish as well as classic international films in their original language. Most of the city's cinemas take part.

Christmas and New Years

Leading up to Christmas – which is celebrated Christmas Eve – the city is aglow with festive lights and decorations, and *gløgg* and *æbleskiver* (a version of mulled wine and dough balls with apple inside) is sold everywhere. On New Year's Eve Rådhuspladsen is the scene of a massive fireworks fest, champagne drinking and kissing of strangers.

Danish

In general, English is widely understood throughout Denmark, as is German, and young people especially often speak both fluently. However, even with little need to resort to Danish, learning a few phrases will surprise and delight any Danes you meet. If you can speak Swedish or Norwegian, then you should have little problem making yourself understood – all three languages share the same root.

There is no single word in the Danish language for "please". So when a Dane doesn't say "please" when speaking to you in English, it's not because they're rude – the word just doesn't come naturally. Danes are also renowned for being direct – if they want something they say "Give me..." – which can, incorrectly, be interpreted as impolite.

An idea of pronunciation for key phrases is given in brackets below.

Basic words and phrases
Taler de engelsk? (tayla dee ENgellsg) Do you speak English?
Ja (ya) Yes
Nej (nye) No
Jeg forstår det (yai fus TO day igge) I don't understand**ikke**
Værså venlig (verso venli) Please (or the nearest thing to)
Tak (tagg) Thank you
Undskyld (unsgul) Excuse me
Hi (hye) Hello/Hi
Godmorgen (goMORN) Good morning
Goddag (goDA) Good afternoon
Godnat (goNAD) Goodnight
Farvel (faVELL) Goodbye
Hvor er? (voa ea?) Where is?
Hvad koster det? (vath kosta day?) How much does it cost?
Jeg vil gerne ha... (yai vay GERna ha) I'd like...
Hvor er toiletterne? (voa ea toaLETTaneh?) Where are the toilets?
Et bord til ... (et boa te...) A table for...
Må jeg bede om regningen? (moah yai beyde uhm RYningan?) Can I have the bill/check, please?
Billet (billed) Ticket

Food and drink basics
Bøfsandwich Hamburger
Brød Bread
Det kolde bord Help-yourself cold buffet
Is Ice cream
Ostebord Cheese board
Peber Pepper
Pølser Frankfurters/sausages
Rugbrød Rye bread
Salt Salt
Sildebord A selection of spiced and pickled herring
Kylling Chicken
Oksekød Beef
Svinekød Pork
Kartofler Potatoes
Fisk Fish
Smør Butter
Smørrebrød Open sandwiches
Sukker Sugar
Wienerbrød "Danish" pastry
Øl Beer
Fadøl Draught beer
Guldøl Strong beer
Vin Wine
Husets vin House wine
Hvidvin White wine
Rødvin Red wine
Mineralvand Mineral water
Chokolade (varm) Chocolate (hot)
Kærnemælk Buttermilk
Kaffe (med fløde) Coffee (with cream)
Mælk Milk
Te Tea
Vand Water

Chronology

1043 The name "Havn" appears in the Knýtlinga Saga, described as the place Norwegian king Magnus sought cover after being defeated at sea.

1160 Bishop Absalon is given control over "Havn" by his foster brother King Valdemar. Recent excavations have shown that Copenhagen at the time was a significant fishing village – Kongens Nytorv largely built on fish bones – and its residents unusually tall.

1167 Bishop Absalon completes the construction of fortified Københavns Slot on present day's Slotholmen Island. Its aim is to protect the town's fishermen and traders from Wendish pirates.

1238 The construction of the town's first monastery commences – today's Helligåndshus.

1249 The earliest recorded attack and plunder of the town by a Hanseatic fleet from Lübeck.

1334 With 5000 inhabitants Copenhagen is Scandinavia's largest settlement.

1369 The town is attacked and briefly occupied by Hanseatic forces who systematically dismantle Københavns Slot.

1417 King Eric of Pomerania makes the newly reconstructed Københavns Slot his seat of power and residence of the royal family.

1443 Copenhagen replaces Roskilde as Denmark's capital.

1479 Copenhagen University, the first in Scandinavia, is established in today's Latin Quarter.

1536 Protestant Reformation takes hold with the arrest of the Catholic Bishop of Copenhagen.

1588 Christian IV aka "The Builder King" is born. After taking the throne at the age of ten he begins a lifelong programme of works. Among his many feats are the neighbourhood of Christianshavn, the city's defensive ring of moats, ramparts and Kastellet, Rosenborg Slot and Rundetårn.

1657 Skåne is ceded to Sweden at the Treaty of Roskilde, Denmark's second most important town Malmö thereby becoming Swedish.

1659 After three years' siege, the city is stormed by Swedish troops.

1660 Absolute monarchy is introduced.

1711 Plague epidemic kills at least 22,000.

1728 The first "great fire" of Copenhagen destroys over a thousand buildings

1730 Christian VI decides to have Københavns Slot torn down and a much grander Louis XIV Rococo-style palace – renamed Christiansborg – is erected in its stead. It burns to the ground 28 years after its completion in 1766. Only the stables and riding ground survive.

1795 The second great fire of Copenhagen burns Christiansborg to the ground.

1801 British and Danish ships engage at the Battle of Copenhagen. Horatio Nelson famously turns a blind eye to Admiral Sir Hyde Parker's orders to retreat.

1807 Fearing the Danes may side with Napoleon, the Royal Navy shells Copenhagen. After three nights of bombardment, large parts of the city lie in ruins. The Danish-Norwegian navy is surrendered to the British.

1828 A new Romanesque-style Christiansborg is completed.

1836 Hans Christian Andersen's *The Little Mermaid* is published.

1838 Sculptor Bertel Thorvaldsen returns to Copenhagen after forty years in Rome.

1843 George Carstensen's brainchild Tivoli opens in the former rampart area.

1843 Father of Existentialism Søren Kierkegaard's *Either/Or* is published.

1847 J.C. Jacobsen founds the Carlsberg brewery.

1884 The second Christiansborg is burnt to the ground leaving only Christiansborgs Slotskirke standing.

1897 The Ny Carlsberg Glyptotek is opened by philanthropic brewing magnate Carl Jacobsen, son of J.C.

1911 The National Romantic Central Station stands completed.

1913 The Little Mermaid statue by Edvard Eriksen (and paid for by Carl Jacobsen) is unveiled.

1928 The current neo-Baroque Christiansborg is completed.

1940 In the early hours of April 9, Copenhagen is occupied by German forces with barely a shot fired.

1943–1945 Most of Denmark's Jewish population is smuggled successfully across to Sweden in fishing boats.

1971 First Roskilde festival.

1971 Christiania is founded in disused military barracks on Christianshavn.

1972 Queen Margrethe II ascends the throne.

1973 Denmark joins the EU.

1992 The Danish football team beat Germany to win the European Cup, receiving a heroes' welcome on their return home.

2000 The Øresunds link to Sweden is opened.

2005 Crown Prince Frederik marries his Tasmanian bride Mary.

2007 Copenhagen-based crime drama *The Killing* becomes an international hit (along with its woolly jumpers).

2010 Copenhagen's *Noma* is rated as the world's best restaurant.

2011 Work begins on the new City Circle metro line; construction unearths some remarkable archeological finds.

2012 Copenhagen's first official bicycle super highway opens.

2014 Copenhagen hosts the Eurovision Song Contest in a former shipyard on Papirøen, spending three times its budget.

2016 Copenhagen reaches a milestone, there are official more bicycles than cars in the city.

2019 The City Circle line (M3) opens, marking the largest construction project in Copenhagen during the last 400 years.

SMALL PRINT

Publishing Information
Fourth edition 2020

Distribution
UK, Ireland and Europe
Apa Publications (UK) Ltd; sales@roughguides.com
United States and Canada
Ingram Publisher Services; ips@ingramcontent.com
Australia and New Zealand
Woodslane; info@woodslane.com.au
Southeast Asia
Apa Publications (SN) Pte; sales@roughguides.com
Worldwide
Apa Publications (UK) Ltd; sales@roughguides.com
Special Sales, Content Licensing and CoPublishing
Rough Guides can be purchased in bulk quantities at discounted prices. We can
create special editions, personalised jackets and corporate imprints tailored to
your needs. sales@roughguides.com.
roughguides.com
Printed in China by CTPS

A catalogue record for this book is available from the British Library
The publishers and authors have done their best to ensure the accuracy and
currency of all the information in **Pocket Rough Guide Copenhagen**, however,
they can accept no responsibility for any loss, injury, or inconvenience sustained
by any traveller as a result of information or advice contained in the guide.

Rough Guide Credits
Author: Taraneh Ghajar Jerven
Updater: Robert James Johnsenr
Editor: Siobhan Warwicker
Cartography: Katie Bennett
Managing editor: Rachel Lawrence
Picture editor: Aude Vauconsant
Cover photo research: Sławomir Krajewski

Original design: Richard Czapnik
Senior DTP coordinator: Dan May
Head of DTP and Pre-Press: Rebeka Davies
Layout: Ruth Bradley

Help us update

We've gone to a lot of effort to ensure that this edition of the **Pocket Rough Guide Copenhagen** is accurate and up-to-date. However, things change – places get "discovered", opening hours are notoriously fickle, restaurants and rooms raise prices or lower standards. If you feel we've got it wrong or left something out, we'd like to know, and if you can remember the address, the price, the hours, the phone number, so much the better.

Please send your comments with the subject line "**Pocket Rough Guide Copenhagen Update**" to mail@uk.roughguides.com. We'll credit all contributions and send a copy of the next edition (or any other Rough Guide if you prefer) for the very best emails.

Photo Credits

(Key: T-top; C-centre; B-bottom; L-left; R-right)

Alamy 12B, 14B, 15B, 19C, 19B, 20T, 20C, 32, 36, 42, 43, 81, 82, 105
Anders Bøgild/Copenhagen Media Center 2T
Andreas Wiking/Wiking Fotografi ApS 93
Arken/Copenhagen Media Center 103
Bastard Restaurant 108
Columbus Leth/Aamanns 66
Cristian Alsing/Copenhagen Media Center 41
Daniel Rasmussen/Copenhagen Media Center 2BR
Den_Blaa_Planet 102
Design Museum Denmark 12/13T
Diana Jarvis/Rough Guides 10, 15T, 19T, 20B, 29, 37, 44, 47, 55, 65, 83, 84, 91, 97
Dreamstime 11B, 30, 31, 50, 51, 60, 98, 106
Finn Broendum/Copenhagen Media Center 4
Frank Ronsholt/Zoo Copenhagen 13C
Giuseppe Liverino/Copenhagen Media Center 76
Hanne Fuglbjerg/Copenhagen Media Center 104
Hay House 35
Helena Smith/Rough Guides 6, 16T, 18T, 48, 71, 110/111
iStock 1, 2BL, 21B
Jens Bangsbo/Copenhagen Media Center 63
Jens Markus Lindhe/Copenhagen Media Center 53

Jens Wulff/Den Blå Planet 11T
Kasper Thye/Visit Copenhagen 5
Klaus Bentzen/Copenhagen Media Center 21T
La Glace/Copenhagen Media Center 39
La Rocca 68
Marie Louise Munkegaard/Copenhagen Media Center 77
Martin Heiberg/Copenhagen Media Center 17B, 21C
Mikkeller 87
Morten Jerichau/Copenhagen Media Center 14T
Per Anders Jörgensen/Manfreds 94
Per Søgaard/Tolboden 18B
Restaurant Cap Horn/Copenhagen Media Center 56
Roger Norum/Rough Guides 24, 118/119
SALT bar & restaurant 58
Sarah Coghill/Almanak 2CR
Shutterstock 16B, 18C, 22/23, 34
Stilleben 38
Thijs Wolzak/Copenhagen Media Center 101
Ty Stange/Copenhagen Media Center 12/13B, 17T, 26, 28, 69, 74, 89
Ty Stange/Copenhagen Media Center 7
Vespa 59

Cover: Canals of Christiania **Shutterstock**

Index

A

accommodation 112
71 Nyhavn 113
Absalon 114
Admiral Hotel 113
Ansgar 114
Avenue 116
Babette Guldsmeden 114
Cab-Inn City 112
City Hotel Nebo 114
Copenhagen Island 114
CPH Living 114
D'Angleterre 113
Guldsmeden Axel 115
Guldsmeden Bertrams 115
Hotel Central & Café 115
Hotel Nimb 112
Hotel Rye 116
Hotel Sankt Petri 113
Hotel Twentyseven 112
Ibsen 114
Jørgensen 114
Løven 115
Palace Hotel 112
Radisson Blu Royal Hotel 112
Saga Hotel 115
Sct Thomas 115
Sømandshjemmet Bethel 114
The Square 113
Wake Up Copenhagen 115
Zleep Hotel Centrum 115
addresses 122
Amager Strandpark 102
Amagertorv 33
Amalienborg 51
Arbejdermuseet 64
Arken Museum of Modern
Art 103
arrival 120
Assistens Kirkegaard 89
A taste of Torvehallerne 64
Axeltorv Square 27

B

Bakken 98
bars
1105 42
Bang & Jensen 86
Bibendum 68
Blågård's Apotek 95
Bo-Bi Bar 42
Bopa 96
BRUS 96
Café Globen 69
Charlie's Bar 42
Curfew 86
Den Vandrette 59

Falernum 86
Gilt 96
Halvandet 77
Kafe Kapers 96
Kalaset 69
K-Bar 42
Kruts Karport 69
Malmö Brewing Co 109
Märkbar 86
Mello Yello 109
Mesteren & Lærlingen 87
Mikkeller 87
N 96
Nemoland 77
Oak Room 96
Ølbaren 96
Oscar Bar og Café 29
Pixie 97
Props Coffee Shop 97
Ruby 43
Salon 39 87
Sukaiba 105
TAP10 97
The Barking Dog 95
The Living Room 43
Toldboden 59
Vinbaren Vesterbro Torv 87
Vinbodegaen 97
bars (by area)
Christianshavn and Holmen 77
Day-trips 105
Malmö 109
Nørrebro and Østerbro 95
Nyhavn and Frederiksstaden 59
Rosenborg and around 68
Strøget and the Inner City 42
Tivoli and Rådhuspladsen 29
Vesterbro and Frederiksberg 86
Børsen 48
Botanisk Have 61
buses 122
by air 120
by bus and train 120

C

cafés and restaurants
Aamanns 66
Amass 75
Anarki 83
Arken Café 104
ÅrstidErna by the Sea 108
Atlas Bar 38
Bankeråt 67
Bar'Vin 38
Bastard 109
Bento 83

Bevar's 93
Brasserie Nimb 29
Cafe 22 93
Cafe and Ølhalle 67
Café Baaden 104
Café Kystens Perle 104
Café Øieblikket 49
Café Oscar 56
Café Oven Vande 75
Café Siesta 109
Café Sundet 93
Café Sylten 104
Café Viggo 83
Cap Horn 57
Christianshavns Bådudlejning 75
Cofoco 84
Conditori La Glace 38
Copenhagen Street Food 75
DAC Café 75
Dalle Valle 38
Den Franske Café 93
Det Lille Apotek 39
Dolce Sicilia 109
Dragør Røgeri 104
Emmerys 57
Europa 1989 39
Famo 84
Fischer 93
Frk. Barners Kælder 85
Geist 57
Glyptoteket 29
Gourmandiet 94
Granola 85
Grillen 94
Grøften 29
Hansens Gamle Familiehave 85
Høst 67
Ida Davidsen 57
Kadeau 76
Kafferiet 57
Kaffesalonen 94
KanalCafeen 29
Kødbyens Fiskebar 85
Koefoed 67
Kong Hans Kælder 39
Krogs Fiskerestaurant 40
Krua Thai 109
La Galette 40
Lagkagehuset 76
La Rocca 67
Laundromat 94
L'education Nationale 40
Lê Lê Nhà Hang 85
Mad & Kaffe 84
Madklubben Bistro-de-Luxe 57
Madklubben Vesterbro 85
MASH 57

Maven 40
Morgenstedet 76
Mormors 58
Mother 85
Norden 40
Nørrebro Bryghus 95
Nyhavn 17 58
Orangeriet 67
Pakhuskælderen 58
Paludan Bogcafé 40
Paté Paté 86
Paustian 95
Peder Oxe 40
Peter Lieps Hus 104
Pilekælderen 41
Pintxos 67
Rådhuskällaren 109
Rebel 58
Relæ 95
Restaurant Piil & Co 105
Riccos Kaffebar 86
Roast 76
Salt 58
Sebastopol 95
Slotskælderen hos Gitte Kik 41
Slurp Ramen 67
Solde Kafferosteri 109
Søpromenaden 95
Søren K 49
Souls 68
Spicey Kitchen Café 76
Spiseloppen 76
Spisestedet Leonora 105
Spuntino 86
Sticks'n'sushi 68, 86
Sult 41
Taste 58
Torvehallerne 68
Un Mercato 68
Vandkunsten sandwich &
    salatbar 42
Vespa 59
Viva 76
Yaffa 41
cafés and restaurants (by area)
Christianshavn and Holmen 75
Day-trips 104
Malmö 108
Nørrebro and Østerbro 93
Nyhavn and Frederiksstaden
    56
Rosenborg and around 66
Slotsholmen 49
Strøget and the Inner City 38
Tivoli and Rådhuspladsen 29
Vesterbro and Frederiksberg 83
Carlsberg Visitor Centre 80
Central Station 26
Christiania 71, 73
Christiansborg Slotskirke 46
Christianshavn and Holmen 70
Christianshavns Kanal 70

Christians Kirke 70
Chronology 128
cinema 123
clubs
    At Dolores 59
    Sunday 59
clubs (by area)
    Nyhavn and Frederiksstaden
        59
    Rosenborg and around 69
Copenhagen Card 121
crime 123
cycling 122

D
Danish 127
Dansk Arkitektur Center 73
Dansk Jødisk Museum 48
Davids Samling 64
Day-trips 98
Den Blå Planet 102
Den Sorte Diamant 49
Designmuseum Danmark 54
Det Kongelige Teater 34
Dining with the Danes 65
directory A–Z 122
Dragør 103
Dyrehaven 98

E
electricity 123
embassies and consulates 123
emergency numbers 123
Enigma Post & Tele Museum
    91
Experimentarium 91

F
Fælledparken 89
festivals and events 126
    Christmas 126
    Copenhagen Beer Festival 126
    Copenhagen Carnival 126
    Copenhagen Cooking 126
    Copenhagen Jazz Festival 126
    Copenhagen Pride 126
    CPH: PIX 126
    New Years 126
    Roskilde Festival 126
    Sankt Hans Aften 126
Folketing 44
Frederiksberg Have 81
Frederiksberg Slot 81
Frederiksberg Slot 99

G
getting around 120
guided tours 125

H
harbour buses 122
health 123
Helligåndskirken 31
Hirschsprungske Samling 62
Højbro Plads 33
hostels
    Copenhagen Downtown 116
    Danhostel City 116
    Generator 117
    Urban House 117

I
internet 123
Islands Brygge 74
Israels Plads 64
Istedgade 78

K
Kastellet 54
Købmagergade and around 33
Kødbyen 80
Kongens Nytorv 34
Krigsmuseet 47
Kronborg Slot 101
Kunsthal Charlottenborg 50

L
left luggage 123
LGBTQ Copenhagen 124
Lilla Torg 106
lost property 124
Louisiana 98

M
Malmö 106
Malmöhus Castle 106
maps
    Christianshavn and Holmen 72
    Day-trips 100
    Malmö 107
    Nørrebro 88
    Nyhavn and Frederiksstaden 52
    Østerbro 90
    Parkmuseerne 62
    Slotsholmen 46
    Strøget and the Inner City 32
    Tivoli and Rådhuspladsen 25
    Vesterbro and Frederiksberg 80
Maritime Museum of Denmark
    101
Marmorkirken 53
Moderna Muséet 106
money 124
music venues
    Drop Inn 43
    Islands Brygges Kulturhus 77
    Jazzhus Montmartre 43

La Fontaine 43
Loppen 77
Mojo 29
Musikcaféen 43
Rust 97
Vega 87
music venues (by area)
  Christianshavn and Holmen 77
  Nørrebro and Østerbro 97
  Strøget and the Inner City 43
  Tivoli and Rådhuspladsen 29
  Vesterbro and Frederiksberg 87
Musikmuseet 79

N
Nationalmuseet 28
Nørrebro and Østerbro 88
Nyboder 65
Ny Carlsberg Glyptotek 26
Nyhavn 50
Nyhavn and Frederiksstaden 50

O
opening hours 124
Operaen 74

P
Park life 61
phones 124
post 124
public holidays 124

R
Ridebane 45
Rocking Roskilde 99
Rosenborg and around 60
Rosenborg Slot 60
Royal Reception Rooms 44
Royalty Danish style 45
Ruinerne Under Christiansborg 45
Rundetårn 31

S
shops
  Accord 92
  Åhléns City 108

Bang & Olufsen 35
Bruuns Bazaar 35
By Malene Birger 35
Christiania Cykler 75
DAC Bookshop 75
Decadent Copenhagen 35
Designer Zoo 83
DesignMuseum Danmark shop 56
Donn Ya Doll 83
Ecouture by Lund 35
Enula 9 92
Form & Design Center 108
Galerie Asbæk 56
George Jensen 35
Greibe & Kumari 92
Henrik Vibskov 36
Illums Bolighus 36
Jazzcup 36
Karamelleriet 92
Kassandra 36
Keramik og Glasværkstedet 66
Lego 36
Le Klint 36
Løgismose 56
Louis Poulsen 36
Mads Nørgaard 37
Magasin du Nord 37
Melange de Luxe 92
Meyers Deli 83
Munthe 37
Nordatlantens Brygge 75
Normann Copenhagen 92
Paustian 92
Pegasus 66
Peter Beier Chokolade 37
Pour Quoi 92
Radical Zoo 92
Ravnsborggade Antique Stores 92
Royal Copenhagen 37
Samsøe og Samsøe 83
Sögreni of Copenhagen 37
Sømods Bolcher 38
Stig P 38, 93
Stilleben 38
SummerBird 83
Tranquebar 66
Uma Bazaar 108
shops (by area)
  Christianshavn and Holmen 75
  Malmö 108

  Nørrebro and Østerbro 92
  Nyhavn and Frederiksstaden 56
  Rosenborg and around 66
  Strøget and the Inner City 35
  Vesterbro and Frederiksberg 83
Skuespilhuset 53
Slotsholmen 44
smoking 125
Statens Museum for Kunst 61
S-Tog and regular trains 121
Stortorget 106
Strøget 30
Strøget and the Inner City 30

T
taxis 122
The Carlsberg Quarter 79
The Danish Resistance 54
The Latin Quarter 31
The Little Mermaid 55
the metro 121
The Rådhus 27
The Turning Torso 107
Thorvaldsens Museum 47
tickets 121
time 125
tipping 125
Tivoli 24
Tivoli and Rådhuspladsen 24
Torvehallerne 64
tourist information 125
travellers with disabilities 125
travelling with children 126
Tycho Brahe Planetarium 79

V
Vesterbro and Frederiksberg 78
Vesterbrogade 78
Visiting Malmö 107
Vor Frelserskirke 70
Vor Frue Kirke 32

W
What lies beneath, digging up the town 25

Z
Zoologisk Have 82

NOTES

DISCARD